The Unfinished Agenda
for Civil Service Reform

Brookings Dialogues on Public Policy

*The presentations and discussions at Brookings conferences and seminars
often deserve wide circulation as contributions to public understanding
of issues of national importance. The Brookings Dialogues on Public
Policy series is intended to make such statements and commentary
available to a broad and general audience, usually in summary form.
The series supplements the Institution's research publications by
reflecting the contrasting, often lively, and sometimes conflicting views of
elected and appointed government officials, other leaders in public and
private life, and scholars. In keeping with their origin and purpose, the
Dialogues are not subjected to the formal review procedures established
for the Institution's research publications. Brookings publishes them
in the belief that they are worthy of public consideration but does
not assume responsibility for their accuracy or objectivity. And, as
in all Brookings publications, the judgments, conclusions, and
recommendations presented in the Dialogues should not be ascribed to the
trustees, officers, or other staff members of the Brookings Institution.*

The Unfinished Agenda for Civil Service Reform

Implications of the Grace Commission Report

Papers by B. GUY PETERS

EUGENE B. McGREGOR, JR.

EDIE N. GOLDENBERG

BERNARD ROSEN

Edited by CHARLES H. LEVINE

*presented at a conference at the Brookings Institution,
October 15–16, 1984*

THE BROOKINGS INSTITUTION
Washington, D.C.

About Brookings

THE BROOKINGS INSTITUTION is a private nonprofit organization devoted to research, education, and publication in economics, government, foreign policy, and the social sciences generally. Its principal purpose is to bring knowledge to bear on the current and emerging public policy problems facing the American people. In its research, Brookings functions as an independent analyst and critic, committed to publishing its findings for the information of the public. In its conferences and other activities, it serves as a bridge between scholarship and public policy, bringing new knowledge to the attention of decisionmakers and affording scholars a better insight into policy issues. Its activities are carried out through three research programs (Economic Studies, Governmental Studies, Foreign Policy Studies), a Center for Public Policy Education, a Publications Program, and a Social Science Computation Center.

The Institution was incorporated in 1927 to merge the Institute for Government Research, founded in 1916 as the first private organization devoted to public policy issues at the national level; the Institute of Economics, established in 1922 to study economic problems; and the Robert Brookings Graduate School of Economics and Government, organized in 1924 as a pioneering experiment in training for public service. The consolidated institution was named in honor of Robert Somers Brookings (1850–1932), a St. Louis businessman whose leadership shaped the earlier organizations.

Brookings is financed largely by endowment and by the support of philanthropic foundations, corporations, and private individuals. Its funds are devoted to carrying out its own research and educational activities. It also undertakes some unclassified government contract studies, reserving the right to publish its findings.

A Board of Trustees is responsible for general supervision of the Institution, approval of fields of investigation, and safeguarding the independence of the Institution's work. The President is the chief administrative officer, responsible for formulating and coordinating policies, recommending projects, approving publications, and selecting the staff.

Editor's Preface

THIS LATEST volume in the Brookings Dialogues on Public Policy series is the product of a conference entitled The Unfinished Agenda for Civil Service Reform. Participants discussed the personnel recommendations of the Grace Commission report in light of the Civil Service Reform Act of 1978, the personnel practices of other nations, and the practices of private sector firms. They considered advantages and disadvantages of implementing some of the commission's recommendations, including those affecting work force management and federal employees' retirement, salaries, and benefits.

The conference provided a forum for the community of specialists in federal personnel management to discuss avenues of reform raised by the Grace Commission. In the past four years this community has become more politicized and divided, by the interests of the administration, Congress, and employee groups, than at any time in recent years. The Grace Commission's personnel recommendations provided the opportunity to bring together these adversarial groups along with interested persons from academic, business, and public interest organizations in the hope of achieving some consensus about directions for reform. As evidenced by the depth of disagreement at the conference, a consensus still seems well out of reach. These essays, however, contribute to the debate by clarifying the important issues and constraints involved in any future attempt at civil service reform.

The Brookings Institution is grateful to the J. M. Foundation and the U.S. Office of Personnel Management for sponsoring the conference, which was held on October 15 and 16, 1984. A. Lee Fritschler, Barbara D. Littell, James M. Mitchell, John Post, and

Roger D. Semerad helped to plan the conference, and Angela M. Specht provided assistance. Theresa B. Walker edited the manuscript, and Chisolm B. Hamilton prepared it for typesetting. Janet Garry provided research assistance.

Charles H. Levine
Editor

April 1985
Washington, D.C.

Contents

CHARLES H. LEVINE
Introduction   **1**
General Discussion   15

B. GUY PETERS
Administrative Change and the Grace Commission   **19**
General Discussion   40

EUGENE B. McGREGOR, JR.
**The Grace Commission's Challenge
to Public Personnel Administration**   **43**
General Discussion   60

EDIE N. GOLDENBERG
**The Grace Commission and Civil Service Reform:
Seeking a Common Understanding**   **69**
General Discussion   95

BERNARD ROSEN
**Civil Service Reform:
Are the Constraints Impenetrable?**   **102**
General Discussion   115

**Appendix: A Summary of the Personnel Report
of the Grace Commission**   **121**

Conference Participants   **140**

Introduction

CHARLES H. LEVINE

NO ONE, it seems, is happy with the present state of the federal government's personnel system, perhaps least of all the Grace Commission and its chairman, J. Peter Grace. Established through an executive order by President Reagan on June 30, 1982, as the President's Private Sector Survey on Cost Control (Grace Commission), its mandate was to identify opportunities for increasing efficiency and reducing cost in the federal government. One of the major opportunities investigated was the cost of the federal work force; the commission proposed changes in the federal personnel system that it estimated would save $90.9 billion (out of $424.4 billion in overall savings) during the first three years after implementation.[1] Although the commission has had its critics, and much disagreement has arisen about the accuracy of its figures and the value of some of its specific recommendations, there is less disagreement about the seriousness of the issues raised by the commission. Virtually everyone who is knowledgeable about the federal personnel system—public managers, unions and employee associations, personnel specialists, members of Congress and their staffs, researchers, and the Reagan administration—can point to dysfunctional aspects of the present system and can recommend avenues for improvement. The central problem for reform, however, is that there is little consensus on the parts of the system that are dysfunctional and on the changes that will lead to various kinds of improvements.

The irony of this situation is that it comes on the heels of a major reform of the civil service system. Six years ago President Carter signed into law the Civil Service Reform Act of 1978, which made sweeping changes in federal personnel management and civil service law.[2] The resulting changes, and some require-

1. President's Private Sector Survey on Cost Control, J. Peter Grace, chairman, *War on Waste* (Macmillan, 1984). *War on Waste* is the commercially published volume that contains the two summary volumes published by the President's Private Sector Survey on Cost Control; and J. Peter Grace, *Burning Money* (Macmillan, 1984).

2. P.L. 95-454 (Oct. 13, 1978). For an analysis of the reform process and early effects of the 1978 act, see Carolyn Ban and Patricia Ingraham, eds., *Legislating Bureaucratic Change* (SUNY Press, 1984).

ments that have yet to be implemented, have come under increasing scrutiny and criticism from those representing public employees and managers. Now, while the initiatives of 1978 are just being reviewed and evaluated, a new set of reform proposals has been presented by the Grace Commission.

The Grace Commission and its personnel recommendations

The task before the Grace Commission required an enormous undertaking. The chairman, J. Peter Grace, recruited 161 members for the executive committee, 80 percent of whom were either chairmen, presidents, chief executive officers, or chief operating officers of some of the nation's largest corporations; they in turn helped to recruit another 2,000 volunteers from the private sector. In all, the commission estimated that the private sector contributed $75 million worth of executive time and support funds to its efforts. The volunteers were organized into thirty-six task forces; of these, twenty-two studied specific departments and agencies and fourteen looked at cross-cutting functions such as personnel, data processing, and procurement. After eighteen months of study, the commission produced forty-seven reports containing 2,478 specific recommendations on 784 different issues. A two-volume, 650-page final summary report was presented to the president on January 16, 1984.

The personnel management task force consisted of twenty-one executives of major U.S. corporations, "recruited to provide a mix of both personnel expertise and experience in general management."[3] The task force identified flaws in the federal personnel management system as a fundamental source of government inefficiency that needed to be attacked in order to substantially reduce program waste. In arriving at its conclusions, the task force reviewed federal personnel policies and practices affecting both civilian and military employees but concentrated primarily on the civilian work force and the Office of Personnel Management (OPM), which administers the laws and regulations governing federal personnel policies and practices.

The method employed by the personnel task force was to (1) gather information concerning the federal personnel system and its impact on government operations through interviews with federal managers at the Office of Personnel Management, the Office of Management and Budget, cabinet-level departments, independent agencies, and the General Accounting Office; (2)

3. President's Private Sector Survey on Cost Control, *Report on Personnel Management* (Washington, D.C.: PPSSCC, 1983), p. 5.

study reports issued by those organizations and the Congressional Budget Office, budget documents and fiscal reports, and statistical data on the federal work force; (3) identify or formulate objectives for each system analyzed; and (4) compare federal personnel operations with those of the private sector by using baseline analyses of various private sector personnel systems covering both personnel practices and costs.[4]

In general, the commission's personnel recommendations were of two types: those to improve work force management, and those to realize cost savings. In pursuit of the former, the task force repeatedly noted the need for interagency cooperation, especially the necessity for the Office of Management and Budget to work more closely with the Office of Personnel Management both in the direct implementation of personnel procedures and, where necessary, in drafting new legislation for Congress. To enhance collaboration and streamlining in work force planning and management, the commission recommended the establishment of a new executive agency, the Office of Federal Management, which would include the Office of Management and Budget, the Office of Personnel Management, the General Services Administration, and other general management functions.

The commission divided its cost savings analysis and recommendations into six categories addressing eighteen separate issues. Appendix A to this introduction summarizes the issues, and appendix B presents three of the commission's most important recommendations on personnel management. As the questions in appendix A imply, the commission's results are quite detailed. The task force report on personnel management covers 351 pages, and the section on personnel management in the final report of the commission covers about 25 percent of the total length of the report. Without getting deeply into details of its findings, it is safe to say that the commission found the federal personnel system costly and dysfunctional in many respects. The appendix at the end of this volume summarizes the commission's findings.

The commission's results have not been met by silence. Critics have charged that the estimates of cost saving were exaggerated and misleading; that the research, analysis, and recommendations were of mixed quality and in some cases inconsistent; and that a "business bias" dominated the results (because a "conflict of interest" occurred when members of some of the task forces had financial interests relating to the study's conclusions; for example,

4. Ibid.

the privatization of Veterans' Administration hospitals). Critics have also charged that the commission's advice favoring more use of practices in the private sector (including contracting and user fees) indicated that the commission misunderstood the structure and purposes of the federal government. Furthermore, the commission's methodology has been questioned; critics have alleged that the process that the commission followed was overly secretive and hidden from congressional involvement. Finally, it has been argued that the commission greatly underestimated the costs, salaries, and benefits prevailing in the private sector and that by choosing to treat the entire federal establishment as one organization similar to large private firms rather than a cluster of many different types of departments and agencies, the commission made unfair and unreasonable comparisons between the federal government and the private sector.[5]

Despite these criticisms, most knowledgeable observers of the federal personnel system admit that, as presently constituted, it is flawed and, whether or not they agree with the basic purpose and conclusions of the Grace Commission, they can find many recommendations in the report with which they agree. Even the harshest critics of the commission's work agree that some changes are necessary.

Evaluating the Grace Commission's personnel recommendations

To begin to evaluate the commission's activities, findings, and recommendations, five central questions needed to be addressed:

—How well did the Grace Commission understand the changing structure and functions of the federal work force and its personnel system?

—How close did the commission's personnel recommendations come to bringing the federal government's personnel system closer to an ideal state-of-the-art public personnel system?

—How consistent were the commission's personnel recommendations with the purposes and structure set up by the Civil Service Reform Act of 1978?

—How well did the commission understand the process through which major personnel reform can be accomplished?

5. U.S. Congressional Budget Office and U.S. General Accounting Office, *Analysis of the Grace Commission's Major Proposals for Cost Control* (Government Printing Office, 1984); *Report of the Task Force on Personnel Management of the President's Private Sector Survey on Cost Control,* Hearing before the Subcommittee on Investigations of the House Committee on Post Office and Civil Service, 98 Cong. 1 sess. (GPO, 1983); Laurie McGinley, "Touted Report Won't Be Heeded," *Wall Street Journal,* November 30, 1984, p. 64; and Charles T. Goodsell, "The Grace Commission: Seeking Efficiency for the Whole People?" *Public Administration Review,* vol. 44 (May–June, 1984), pp. 196–204.

—How was the commission's report viewed by the Reagan administration, especially by the Office of Personnel Management?

To set the stage for the discussion of these questions at a conference at the Brookings Institution, four knowledgeable scholars were invited to prepare essays on these issues. The essays and the general discussions of each follow this introduction.

The first question is addressed by B. Guy Peters. By drawing from data on the federal work force since 1968 and developments in Europe during the past decade, especially those in Great Britain, Peters concludes that the Grace Commission may have over-estimated the extent to which similarities exist between the work forces of the federal government and the private sector. Citing the increased professionalization and specialization of the federal work force, he argues that government is becoming more knowl-edge-intensive and less labor-intensive than the private sector, and thus comparisons between them are inappropriate. The author also cites the shrinking payrolls and perquisites of the federal work force in comparison with those of the private sector as a dangerous sign for maintaining the labor market competitiveness of the federal government. Further, he points out that the civil service system has evolved into a system of "arrangements," a trend toward a loosely related set of different groups of people working for the federal government, rather than toward a more integrated civil service system. Such fragmentation, while re-sponsive to different agencies' needs and labor markets, threatens the integrity and logic of the existing civil service system. Finally, the author identifies the increased politicization and unionization of the federal work force, which on the one hand serve to destabilize and on the other create rigidities in the system that preclude effective work force performance.

Peters finds that the commission was insensitive to some of these developments, particularly in its emphasis on the growth and costs of the federal work force. He concludes that the commission and its recommendations could not have come at a more inopportune time. He cautions that the commission's report and its recommendations, if implemented, may cut costs but are bound to hurt morale, recruitment, and retention, which in turn are likely to negatively affect the quality of government services.

The second question—whether the commission's personnel recommendations advance the federal personnel system toward a state-of-the-art system—is addressed by Eugene B. McGregor, Jr. McGregor concludes that the Grace Commission put its finger on a serious problem of federal management; that is, even though the federal government has a sophisticated system of operational rules and procedures, governmentwide work force management does not exist. In his view, the state-of-the-art challenge in personnel administration is not a matter of achieving a higher level of operational sophistication, but revolves around how personnel operations and strategic management can be linked.

This key insight of the commission's work, however, is followed by what McGregor terms "standard pleas for eliminating waste. . . . a standard fare of 'volume up, costs down' recommendations that public managers have come to expect from the business community." Although he dismisses the commission's recommendations as overblown estimates of cost savings or as inappropriate major changes in public policy, the author urges a more positive approach; that is, to take seriously some of the commission's recommendations on governmentwide work force management. The present lack of reliable information about the federal work force, according to McGregor, makes it impossible to determine if the conclusions of the commission about the excessive size and cost of the federal work force are accurate. What the commission has documented is the extent of the federal government's ignorance about its own operation. The president's survey of the private sector "could not be more discriminating in its analysis," the author argues, "because federal managers do not themselves have the data that would demonstrate the adequacy or inadequacy of their own practices."

McGregor's essay then addresses the absence of a management office in government concerned with linking program goals and staffing requirements. He observes that there is a set of work force management functions related to a managerial view of human resources that is not now the concern of either the Office of Personnel Management or the Office of Management and Budget. If these functions, which are quite consistent with some of the logic of the commission's recommendations, were incorporated into government, the savings forecasted by the commission may actually seem small by comparison with the long-term savings gained from making government work force management more effective.

The third question—how the commission's findings and recommendations squared with the purpose and structure set up by the Civil Service Reform Act of 1978—was tackled by Edie N. Goldenberg. She examines three goals common to both the Grace Commission and the 1978 act: (1) attracting and retaining the best executive talent, (2) giving federal managers the necessary tools to manage well, and (3) strengthening the place of research, demonstration projects, and program evaluation in the federal government. She then questions a central assumption of the commission's endeavor—that the strategies and experience of the private sector can and should be adopted by the public sector.

After providing an extensive review of the results of the 1978 act and comparing them with some of the assumptions and recommendations of the commission, Goldenberg reaches several important conclusions. First, changing personnel management in the federal government takes time and requires sustained leadership in a consistent direction. When political leadership changes frequently, reforms are often judged prematurely and sometimes reversed before they have sufficient time to have an effect. For that reason, the author believes that the commission's proposal to shift responsibility for leadership in personnel management from the Office of Personnel Management to an Office of Federal Management is premature. Second, morale and trust are eroded by promoting unrealistic expectations among employees about the financial gains that might flow from personnel policy changes. She observes that unrealized financial gains from the 1978 act have fostered employee cynicism that threatens other management improvement efforts. Third, calculating benefit-cost ratios for personnel management reforms in the public sector is a complex undertaking. Short-term and direct dollar savings can easily be exaggerated and overvalued when compared with long-term indirect savings and with long-term costs in program equity, government responsiveness, and individual liberty. Finally, Goldenberg argues that systematic experimentation and study are essential before massive changes in the federal personnel system are introduced throughout the government. Even though the principle of experimentation through demonstration projects is written into the 1978 act, the demonstration authority is underutilized, and evaluation of personnel management programs is underemphasized.

Goldenberg concludes that the complexity of management in the public sector and the diversity of its circumstances require deliberateness in establishing a foundation for governmentwide change. She also cautions that management concepts taken from the private sector are worth considering, but only after they have been adjusted appropriately for the special purposes of the public sector.

The fourth question—how well the commission understood the process through which major personnel reform can be accomplished—is addressed by Bernard Rosen. Rosen argues that the behavior of the Grace Commission makes it unlikely that it will be able to overcome some persistent constraints on reforming the federal personnel system. Indeed, Rosen argues that the commission may have made some general constraints into possibly impenetrable barriers.

Rosen's paper examines four of these general constraints: political reality, credibility of the reform effort, legal requirements, and administrative uncertainty. He focuses on the Grace Commission's shortcomings in each of these areas and proposes three "late-course corrections" to facilitate action on recommendations that are well supported by facts. He suggests first, that the commission should put aside or modify unsupported recommendations and the accompanying discussion in accordance with the facts; second, that the commission should inform the president of the changes; and third, that J. Peter Grace and his associates should stop misinforming the American people with erroneous oral and written statements about the pay and benefits of federal employees.

Rosen argues that such an approach would "clear the poisoned air sufficiently to make possible a new constructive dialogue" with Congress and employee organizations. He concludes by cautioning that such a dialogue is not likely to occur if the advocates of change insist on discussing each proposal in isolation from other considerations. Changes in the retirement system, for example, must be linked to pay adjustments that make federal wages competitive with large corporations in order to recruit and retain competent employees. Rosen observes that a dialogue about comparability based on grounds of total compensation could provide a new opportunity for sensible compromises and might be the surest road to significant legislative changes in federal personnel policy.

The last question—how the commission's report was received by the Reagan administration—was addressed by Herbert E. Ellingwood, chairman of the Merit Systems Protection Board, and by Donald J. Devine, director of the Office of Personnel Management. Ellingwood said that no matter what the outcome of deliberations over the Grace Commission's recommendations in the executive and legislative branches, he could predict with certainty that issues will develop that must be resolved within the court system. The Merit Systems Protection Board, as an administrative quasi-judicial agency, undoubtedly will be part of that process, either through adjudication of the related appeals it will receive or through review of the validity of rules and regulations issued by the Office of Personnel Management to implement any laws enacted by Congress. Although Ellingwood's involvement in the legal matters that are likely to arise out of the commission's recommendations prohibited him from addressing some details of the report, he pointed out that many principles developed by the personnel management task force of the Grace Commission are entirely compatible with the merit system's statutory protections and probably would be compatible with the personal beliefs of most federal employees.

Citing the task force's Start Work Statement and comparing it with the merit principles, Ellingwood said that to the extent that the Merit Systems Protection Board can and does have an institutional view of the Grace Commission's recommendations, it can best be stated as an adherence to and a belief in the desirability of conducting the affairs of government according to the principles of sound business and fiscal management, and a guarantee to insure the worth and dignity of the individual. Ellingwood said that from the viewpoint of an agency manager, albeit a small agency of 380 employees, it is necessary to increase incentives for qualified people to enter and remain in government and to give managers the tools they need to operate effectively. He felt the commission recognized that need. Citing some conclusions of studies conducted by the Merit Systems Protection Board, Ellingwood pointed out that several of the commission's recommendations reached similar conclusions, for example, giving greater priority to performance in retaining employees in reduction-in-force situations. Ellingwood concluded by observing that changes in the federal government's personnel management system, whether carefully planned or not, are inevitable; the Grace Commission's recommendations are a useful catalyst for deciding on a positive course of action.

Devine addressed the subject of what the Office of Personnel Management is doing to implement the Grace Commission's recommendations. He began by pointing out that arguing over the exactness of the figures in the report is simply a means of diverting attention from the recommendations—which are excellent and would save billions of dollars. He pointed out that 17 percent of the federal budget is accounted for by operating and management expenses. About $100 billion is spent on personnel alone. He added that the Reagan administration had already begun to reap savings before the commission's recommendations and that the commission has added more ideas. Devine cited several initiatives of the Office of Personnel Management consistent with the Grace Commission's recommendations: tightening up on disability retirements, initiation of planning to help reduce the "bulge" of middle management positions in government, proposed changes in regulations pertaining to reductions in force to give greater reward for performance, establishment of a work force management division, consolidation of supervisory training courses, the establishment of guidelines for public notification of job openings, and greater use of the Government Incentives Awards Act.

Devine asserted that since 1981 the Office of Personnel Management saved taxpayers $18 billion by making these and other sound business decisions. He added that to make appreciably greater savings of the sort proposed by the Grace Commission will require the cooperation of Congress. He concluded by observing how difficult that would be in the area of retirement and how difficult it had been to achieve a compromise with Congress on the retention-based-on-performance system for reduction in force.

The search for a new balance   The essays in this volume and the general discussions that follow them suggest that the search for a new balance among the needs of taxpayers, government managers, and employees is a difficult one. The goal of the Grace Commission to redesign the federal government personnel system into a structure that is less costly yet more effective seems to be an illusive target. However, the commission's findings and recommendations and the essays and general discussions of the Brookings conference have identified the general factors that are likely to be incorporated in any reforms of the civil service system. They include cost issues, like the pay, perquisites, and pensions of federal employees, and issues of work force management and employee motivation and morale.

The feasibility of reforming the civil service system also came under scrutiny at the conference. Questions were raised about the composition, findings, and behavior of the commission itself, especially about the likelihood that a group of business people could launch a reform effort aimed at changing the federal personnel system. The conference revealed that in the remainder of the 1980s, improving human resource management in the federal government is likely to be a more achievable objective than significantly realigning the compensation equation.

History has shown that when a consensus emerges around an administrative doctrine that promises both effective public management and fair wages and benefits, significant reform is possible.[6] Without this consensus, reform is likely to be achieved only under the most strained political conditions. The Brookings conference and this volume show clearly that, at least for now, such a doctrine and consensus are far from emerging. Indeed, the papers reveal the depth of many of the disagreements among the groups that make up the public personnel policy community. On a more positive note, it should be recognized that through discussion of the Grace Commission and its report, the conference clarified many of the participants' positions on policy issues and perhaps contributed to the modification of others. At a minimum, it served to define critical factors that will have to be incorporated into any future effort to improve the federal government's personnel management system.

6. See, for example, Ronald C. Moe, *The Hoover Commissions Revisited* (Westview Press, 1982); and Alan K. Campbell, "Civil Service Reform as a Remedy for Bureaucratic Ills," in Carol H. Weiss and Allen H. Barton, eds., *Making Bureaucracies Work* (Sage Publications, 1979), pp. 153–66.

Appendix A: A Summary of Personnel Issues

Federal Employee Benefits System

Retirement systems. Are retirement benefits overly liberal, and do they serve as an incentive to early retirement?

Health insurance. Can the federal employees health benefit program be made more cost effective while still maintaining adequate coverage?

Annual leave. Can costs of vacation time be reduced by amending the annual leave policy to conform with private sector practices?

Sick leave. Can sick leave costs be reduced by making sick leave policy conform more closely with that in the private sector?

Federal Position Classification System

Position classification. Are there excessive costs due to overgrading, and can administrative costs be reduced? Can individual agencies be held more accountable for position management?

Compensation and Classification System

Pay comparability. Is pay comparability, as currently structured, a sound approach for the federal sector?

Note. The information in appendix A is based on the President's Private Sector Survey on Cost Control, *Report on Personnel Management* (Washington, D.C.: PPSSCC, 1983).

Blue-collar pay comparability. Is the federal wage system designed and administered so that pay comparability is achieved as intended?

Executive level and Senior Executive Service pay. Is the current method of setting pay appropriate for the executive and Senior Executive Service levels? Is the "pay cap" for federal career executives a serious disincentive for continued service?

Personnel Management Operations

The employment process and public information. Can the Office of Personnel Management modify the process of providing public information about job openings in order to reduce the number of inquiries and limit it to those applicants reasonably suitable and qualified for available positions? Will restricting the number of applicant inquiries adversely affect the quality of applicants for certification?

The employment process and automated examining. Should the Office of Personnel Management assign priority to the control and development of "distributed automated examining systems"?

Reductions in force. Would modifications to the current reduction-in-force procedures reduce disruption, lower costs, and preserve the quality of the work force without adversely affecting employee rights?

Permanent employment versus contracted services. Can federal functions that are commercial in nature be contracted out to the private sector at a lesser cost?

Training and Development Services

Instructional television production facilities. Should the Office of Personnel Management act as "broker" to coordinate utilization of the approximately twenty-five separate government-operated television studios in the Washington, D.C.-Baltimore area?

Duplication of supervisory training. Would more centrally controlled and guided management training programs under the Office of Personnel Management result in better quality and lower cost?

Executive seminar center operations. Can current operating costs of the Office of Personnel Management's executive seminar centers be reduced through improved productivity and more efficient use of facilities?

Organization Planning and Productivity

Productivity. Should the federal government establish a central office designated to promote and coordinate formal, visible programs for productivity improvements throughout its operations?

Duplication of personnel services. Can federal agencies consolidate certain personnel offices and services?

Work force planning. Should the federal government have a uniform work force planning method for use within the agencies?

Appendix B: Major Personnel Findings and Recommendations

Work Force Management

Findings. The Grace Commission found serious deficiencies in the planning for and use of the federal work force. These deficiencies are apparent in overstaffing, lack of employee motivation, and low productivity. The problems are deep-rooted in the lack of a management structure to focus on human resource needs.

Recommendations. The Office of Personnel Management should develop a systematic approach to formulating human resource policies and procedures for use by all government agencies to insure the application of high standards of personnel development.

Retirement Systems

Findings. The commission reviewed the two largest federal retirement systems, the civil service retirement system and the military retirement system, which together cover approximately 98 percent of government employees, and the foreign service retirement system. The conclusion was that the government retirement plans provide benefits and incur costs three to six times as great as the best plans in the private sector.

The commission also found that, in general, the three retirement systems investigated specify benefit formulas more liberal than can typically be found in the private sector; allow retirement, with unreduced benefits, at an earlier age than is typically found in the private sector; and provide full protection against inflation.

Recommendations. Federal retirement costs should be reduced to levels comparable to those in the private sector by increasing the normal retirement age from age fifty-five for the civil service and about forty for the military to age sixty-two, reducing benefits actuarially for retirement before age sixty-two, reducing the credit granted for each year of service to levels comparable to those in the private sector, revising the benefit formula to define base

Note. The information in appendix B is compiled from the President's Private Sector Survey on Cost Control, *A Report to the President,* vol. 1 (Washington, D.C.: PPSSCC, 1983), pp. 258, 280, 304.

earnings as the average of the highest five years' salary (versus three years currently), and revising cost-of-living adjustments to reflect prevailing private sector practices. Smaller pension plans (including foreign service retirement) should be revised to be consistent with those of the civil service retirement system.

Health and Other Fringe Benefits

Findings. The federal government spent approximately $45.5 billion on fringe benefits for executive branch civilian personnel in 1982, 68.2 percent of total payroll costs. By 1987, fringe benefits are projected to be 70.6 percent of total payroll. The commission compared the costs and controls of federal fringe benefits and of standard practices regarding benefits in the private sector and concluded that mismanagement, inefficiencies, and abuse have led to excessive costs in the federal system. In addition, the policies of the federal government on health benefits and on vacation and sick pay are more liberal than comparable standards in the private sector. Further, procedures and controls of the federal government are inadequate to detect fraud and abuse in disability benefits. Military health benefits and the military health care system also need to improve efficiency in order to eliminate excess capacity, introduce cost-containment measures, and coordinate health resources planning.

Recommendations. The costs of federal fringe benefits must be reduced by eliminating benefits that exceed prevailing practices in the private sector, by introducing cost-containment provisions in health plans, and by deliberalizing vacation and sick pay provisions. The costs of military health benefits can be reduced by providing central coordination of health care systems and limiting access to nonmilitary hospitals; these changes would increase utilization of military health care facilities.

General Discussion

THE CONFERENCE began with a presentation by J. P. Bolduc, senior vice-president of W. R. Grace and Company and former chief operating officer of the President's Private Sector Survey on Cost Control. Bolduc outlined the basic strategy of the Grace Commission's work and some of its major findings. He began with a discussion of the national deficit and the importance of the commission's recommendations in reducing it. He pointed out that of the commission's 2,478 recommendations, 73 percent required congressional action and 27 percent could be implemented by the executive branch (although that figure is realistically more like 10 to 12 percent, given congressional prohibitions on certain actions of the executive branch).

Bolduc mentioned several problems in the way the federal government handles its accounting and information systems. He pointed out that the government has 332 incompatible accounting systems and that the lack of reliable, accurate, and comprehensive data makes it difficult for people to agree on the magnitude of problems or the efficacy of alternatives. An example he noted was the size of the national debt, which he estimated at $4.5 trillion (not the $1.5 trillion usually mentioned) when one adds off-budget items like unfunded liability for military and civil service pensions. Bolduc said that the federal government has 319 different payroll systems and wondered why federal employees are not paid according to one unified, consistent, fully integrated and compatible payrolling system.

Bolduc emphasized that the purpose of the commission was not to "pick on" federal employees but to find potential opportunities for cost savings throughout government. He said the commission found some quite competent, capable, and dedicated federal employees who could do a service and work very effectively in the private as well as the public sector.

In Bolduc's view, increased taxes are an ineffective way to reduce the deficit; he believed that cost cutting would yield substantial deficit reductions. As examples, he mentioned reducing the overlap and duplication in personnel offices and improving the handling of sick leave and annual leave, the pay comparability study, and position classification. He also referred to an overgenerous retirement system for civil service and military retirees, a plan that he said is three to six times more generous than the best private sector plan, largely because of the full cost-of-living adjustment for government retirees and the early age at which government employees are eligible to retire.

To support and promote implementation of the Grace Commission's recommendations, Bolduc said that J. Peter Grace and others have formed a foundation called "Citizens Against Waste"—a broad-based, bipartisan organization whose basic purpose is to inform and mobilize the American people to speak out. The foundation has three basic objectives: to educate the American people; to organize a petition demanding action on waste and inefficiency, which the foundation hopes will be signed by 50 million persons and delivered to the president and Congress; and to seek memberships to demonstrate that this is not a short-term effort but rather an ongoing one with continuity.

A. Lee Fritschler, director of Brooking's Advanced Study program, pointed out that the Grace Commission report had been criticized by some for containing significant statistical errors. Bolduc responded that Fritschler was correct, that some commission data have been questioned by Congress and the Congressional Budget Office. He said, however, that the numbers in question were not challenged because of what the commission calculated, but because it drew on different sources of information owing to the way government maintains its records. He mentioned in particular the issue of the Congressional Budget Office's confirming only $98.7 billion of the savings that the commission said would occur during a three-year period following the implementation of its recommendations. What has not been reported by the media, he said, is that the Congressional Budget Office only looked at 11 percent of the recommendations and did not include the recommendations whose value was less than $1 billion in savings.

Jerry Klepner, staff director of the House Subcommittee on Compensation and Employee Benefits, said that Bolduc had given an erroneous impression of civil service retirement. He pointed out that the average retirement age for employees in the private sector is sixty-two years, and the average retirement age for employees in the federal government is sixty-one plus years. There is a difference of only seven months between the average

age in those two sectors. Bolduc responded to Klepner's point by saying that one has to be careful when dealing with averages. He said that the average retirement age in the private sector is sixty-three, not sixty-two, and furthermore, that when employees retire early in the private sector, they are given a significantly reduced percentage of the total benefits that would accrue to them; that does not happen in the public sector if one retires at age fifty-five with thirty years of service or at age sixty with twenty years of service. The key point is that one simply cannot cite a typical age or an average age without looking at the benefits that accrue to that individual at the time of retirement. Klepner replied that he was simply addressing Bolduc's statement about average retirement age in the public and private sectors, not the level of benefits, because it is an important issue but nevertheless a different one.

Duncan Bailey, former deputy director for research and economics of the President's Private Sector Survey on Cost Control, said that if one takes as a base the total number of civil service retirees in 1982, the average retirement age was fifty-eight and a half years. Bolduc added that 26 percent of those on federal retirement today retire as a result of disability, and the average disability retirement age, he believes, is fifty-three and a half.

Ronald Moe, a specialist in American government for the Congressional Research Service, said that one of the criticisms of the commission's work was the relative lack of sophistication of its report and the fact that the rules of the game are so different between the public and private sectors that the unique needs of the public sector were not recognized by the commission. Moe pointed out that the issue of where a function should be performed involves more than money and short-term savings. He said that there are many good reasons for Congress to proceed carefully with regard to privatization. Bolduc responded that there are 500,000 jobs in the federal government with functions that are similar to those in commercial business. Thousands of those government jobs have been recommended to Congress for contracting out, but that has not occurred. One of the biggest problems identified by the Grace Commission is that there is no accounting for overhead costs in the federal government; data on the true costs are simply not available.

Earl Armbrust, deputy assistant director for general government in the Congressional Budget Office, sought to clarify the issue of coverage by the joint report issued by the General Accounting Office and the Congressional Budget Office. He pointed out that while the joint study had a $1 billion cutoff for analyzing recommendations, in terms of dollars, it covered 90 percent of the estimated savings. He said that from a dollar-weighted point of view, the joint analysis covered a large part of the total recommendations. Bolduc replied that part of the problem is the way the budget is prepared on the basis of authority, obligations, and outlays, and that the numbers the commission relied upon represented the total cost of operation, not the part that appears in the budget after offsetting receipts have been added.

Armbrust said that he realizes that the government has multiple systems but the basic way that information is presented is in terms of budget deficits—the difference between total cash in and total cash out. Bolduc asked Armbrust if he would acknowledge that such a perspective is an inadequate representation of the financial status of the country. Armbrust replied that for now the best way to present any recommendations is within the framework of the deficits faced in the Congress and the kind of policy choices it must make. Armbrust added that he thought the current accounting system provides a fair notion of what the annual cost is.

Administrative Change and the Grace Commission

B. GUY PETERS

THE CIVIL SERVICE, or "the bureaucracy," has become a target for almost any group in society that is displeased with the government. In Herbert Kaufman's words, fear of bureaucracy has become a "raging pandemic."[1] Those on the ideological Right charge that the bureaucracy is composed of slothful, inefficient, and wasteful paper pushers. Those on the ideological Left criticize the commitment of the bureaucracy to middle class values and allege that poor treatment of clients results from those commitments.[2] This hostility causes difficulty for civil servants, especially the managers in the civil service, who must maintain motivation and commitment in the face of so much vituperation. The stereotype of the public employee also belies the truth, for the large majority of career civil servants appear to have at least the same levels of motivation and commitment as their private sector counterparts.[3]

Although perhaps more apparent in the United States during the Reagan administration, criticism of the civil service is not new. President Richard M. Nixon tried to reorganize the bureaucracy to maximize the power of his (and subsequent presidents') appointees over the career civil service.[4] President Jimmy Carter used criticism of Washington and the civil service as a major component of his campaign in 1976, and his reforms of the civil service reflected a perceived need to change the structures of the civil service and its methods of management. He wanted to develop a personnel system more similar to those systems in the private sector.

The author gratefully acknowledges the support for this research by a Hallsworth Fellowship at the Department of Government at the University of Manchester.

1. Herbert Kaufman, "Fear of Bureaucracy: A Raging Pandemic," *Public Administration Review,* vol. 41 (Jan.–Feb., 1981), pp. 1–9.

2. B. Guy Peters, *The Politics of Bureaucracy,* 2d ed. (New York: Longman, 1983).

3. Charles Goodsell, *The Case for Bureaucracy* (Chatham, N.J.: Chatham House, 1983); and H. Brinton Milward and Hal G. Rainey, "Don't Blame the Bureaucracy!" *Journal of Public Policy,* vol. 3 (May 1983), pp. 149–68.

4. Richard P. Nathan, *The Plot That Failed: Nixon and the Administrative Presidency* (John Wiley, 1975).

19

Attacks on the civil service have intensified during the Reagan administration. Reductions in force have occurred in the nondefense departments. For a portion of the civil service the previous merit system of testing for positions has been suspended. Consequently, the merit principle in civil service hiring, promotion, and firing may diminish. Civil service pay and perquisites have eroded to an even greater extent than under previous presidents. By the government's own figures, civil servants are, on average, paid at least 18 percent less than they would be paid in comparable jobs in the private sector. Finally, the President's Private Sector Survey on Cost Control (the Grace Commission) argues that a major cause of the high cost of government is the civil service system, especially the retirement program and the mechanisms for compensation. The Grace Commission estimated that instituting personnel practices more in conformity with practices in the private sector could save the government $90.9 billion in personnel costs over three years.[5]

The United States is not the only country where attacks on the bureaucracy and the presumed privileged position of public sector employees have occurred. Such attacks have been rampant in the United Kingdom under Mrs. Margaret Thatcher's government. Many of the same questions about public personnel—pay comparability, politicization of the civil service, and overly generous, inflation-proofed pensions—are matters of immediate political concern in Britain as well as in the United States. In Britain analyzing public sector management is an ongoing event. These analyses, so-called Rayner exercises (after Sir Derek Rayner, whom Mrs. Thatcher recruited from the Marks and Spencer department store chain), share many characteristics with the Grace Commission. The British analyses, smaller in scale and subject to certain norms about secrecy and the separation of the public and private sectors, have not solicited suggestions for improvement from private sector managers, as the Grace Commission did.[6] In addition, shortly after the initiation of the Rayner exercises, the Thatcher government started another program—the Financial Management Initiative—to introduce many of the practices of private sector management, for example, cost centers, into British

---

5. President's Private Sector Survey on Cost Control, J. Peter Grace, chairman, *War on Waste* (Macmillan, 1984). (Hereafter Grace, *War on Waste*.)

6. Norman Warner, "Raynerism in Practice: Anatomy of a Rayner Scrutiny," *Public Administration,* vol. 62 (Spring 1984), pp. 7–22.

government. The initiative also sought to make central administration more businesslike.[7]

The civil service is also controversial in France and numerous
other European countries. In fact questioning the role of the public
bureaucracy in government, and the rewards to members of the
public service, is an almost universal phenomenon. Because of
that apparent universality, I include some comparisons with the
experience of other countries, especially the United Kingdom, in
this essay.

In this discussion of the federal personnel system and the
implications of the Grace Commission's findings for that system,
I will not concentrate on the problems of estimating monetary
savings that might result from the implementation of the recommendations. The Congressional Budget Office and the General
Accounting Office have done a thorough job of that.[8] Furthermore,
my past involvement with a similar commission at the state level
and with research on such commissions in thirty-four states, leads
me to the conclusion that any estimate of cost saving in government
is an exercise as much in applied theology as in accounting. I will
be looking at the implications of the Grace Commission's recommendations for managing the federal government and its
personnel. The recommendations of the Grace Commission may
save money for the taxpayer, but they may also impose significant
costs on both civil servants and the population as a whole.

The federal civil service in the 1980s

The Grace Commission made its recommendations in the context
of a federal civil service that has changed greatly in the past decade
and that continues to change. Some changes have occurred because
of overt political actions and policies imposed upon the civil
service. Others have evolved as both the tasks performed by
government and the personnel needed to perform those tasks have
changed.

Increasing Professionalization and Specialization

Two significant and somewhat contradictory changes have
occurred in the background and education of the work force of
the federal government. On the one hand, more and more

7. *Efficiency and Effectiveness in the Civil Service,* Cmnd. 8616 (London: Her Majesty's
Stationery Office, 1982); and *Financial Management in Government Departments,* Cmnd. 9058
(London: Her Majesty's Stationery Office, 1983).

8. U.S. Congressional Budget Office and U.S. General Accounting Office, *Analysis
of Grace Commission's Major Proposals for Cost Control* (Government Printing Office, 1984).

professional and technical personnel have been hired; they have skills that are highly marketable in the economy outside government. In addition, they have external professional reference groups. On the other hand, a profession or para-profession of public management has emerged. People trained in that tradition have other public servants as their main reference group, and they expect a career entirely within government. These changes in the professional nature of the personnel in the federal service present challenges for public managers.

The stereotype of the government employee as a paper pusher is decreasingly valid. Certainly the largest single category of employment in the civil service remains clerical personnel. But clerical and secretarial personnel are now likely to have the higher skill levels needed for running office machinery such as word processors. Furthermore, professional and technical employment in the federal government has increased significantly. In 1968, 30.5 percent of the federal white-collar civil service employees were categorized as professional and technical employees. In 1976, the figure was 33.1 percent, and in 1981, 35.6 percent.[9] What is perhaps even more important than the increase in the proportion of federal employees in professional and technical positions is that proportion as compared with the rest of the labor force. In the economy as a whole, only about 10 percent of those employed are employed in professional and technical occupations, while in the civil service more than one-third of the work force is in those types of occupations. A portion of this difference may be the result of the overgrading of some federal jobs. Nevertheless, the federal work force is a comparatively well-educated and qualified one, and consequently many employees can command highly paid and responsible positions in the private economy.

Besides employees with training in established professional and technical occupations, the public service itself has become more established as a profession; the master's in public administration or the master's in public policy serves as the professional credential. Associated with the proliferation of public service professionals has been a proliferation of jobs in staff positions, such as policy analysts and planners, as opposed to positions in the line, service delivery agencies. These professionals are also more likely to be tied into the "issue networks" that surround policymaking in government. Such employees have opinions about how policy

9. U.S. Civil Service Commission, *Occupations of Federal White-Collar Employees* (GPO, various years); and U.S. Bureau of the Census, *Statistical Abstract of the United States, 1983* (GPO, 1984).

should be made in certain areas.[10] They may be less willing than conventional civil servants to be the docile followers of their political masters.

In comparative context, it is interesting that some critics of the civil service in the United Kingdom have suggested removing senior civil servants from their roles as policy advisers. These critics want a civil service system that includes overtly political advisers and managers. Such political executives would change when governments change (just as in the United States). Further, as noted, the Financial Management Initiative stresses the managerial role of the civil servant rather than the role of policy adviser. These moves would alter the professional role of the civil servant in Britain by making the civil servant a manager in a large organization rather than a policy adviser. This role would seem peculiar to the average senior civil servant in Britain but would be, of course, an ordinary one for American civil servants.

Thus government is becoming more knowledge-intensive and less labor-intensive. Increasingly, government employees have professional qualifications that either make them marketable in the private sector or indicate that they have made special preparations for a career in government. That, in turn, makes some of the traditional management practices of the public sector more difficult to sustain. The public manager is no longer working with large numbers of essentially interchangeable parts. Managing a government agency becomes more similar to managing, say, a consulting firm or research organization; each individual within the organization becomes that much more valuable and capable of making a specialized contribution. In addition, the development of professional norms and practices within the public service provides an external reference group, and those standards could present difficulties for a political or career manager who is attempting to behave in less than a professional manner.

Shrinking Pay and Perquisites

Despite the generally increasing qualifications of the federal work force, the pay and perquisites for federal workers have been falling behind those in the private sector for comparable jobs. This fact is widely known in the Washington, D.C., metropolitan area but is perhaps less understood in other parts of the country where federal employment is less dominant in the local economy.

10. Hugh Heclo, "Issue Networks and the Executive Establishment," in Anthony King, ed., *The New American Political System* (Washington, D.C.: American Enterprise Institute, 1978).

The president's pay agent now calculates federal pay, on average, as 18 percent less than pay in comparable jobs in the private sector. The 3.5 percent pay increase scheduled for January 1985 hardly makes up the difference.

The Federal Pay Act of 1970 established comparability of average pay for jobs in the private sector as the basis for setting salaries and wages in the federal government. The act provides for a comparability survey of private employers each year. The president's pay agent can then recommend pay changes that bring federal pay into line with pay in the private sector.[11] The president may accept the recommendations of the comparability exercise, or he may make his own decisions about changes in pay. Numerous technical problems have arisen in the collection and analysis of data used to determine the comparability figures. Critics cite the complicated methodology for calculating the "pay line," the use of whole job comparisons versus job weights, the relatively small number of jobs surveyed, the almost exclusive use of large employers in the private sector, and the exclusion of state and local governments. But within some range of error the survey does produce roughly comparable figures for federal pay. Even the Grace Commission argued that the recommendations were off by only 4 percent.[12] But most presidents have chosen to disregard the recommendations of their pay agents and give the civil service lower wages than recommended. In approximately two-thirds of the years since 1970 the raise granted to federal workers was lower than recommended by the comparability exercise (table 1). According to the 1970 act, presidents can make their own pay policies, and they have chosen to do so. From the perspective of the public employee this system enables a president to score political points at the federal employee's expense.

The comparability (or lack thereof) of federal civil service and private sector pay is not uniform throughout the civil service. Many evaluations show that pay for the lower echelons of the civil service is better than pay for comparable jobs in the private sector, but at the top of the hierarchy, comparability declines drastically.[13] Civil servants at the GS–15 grade earn at least 30 percent less than they would earn in comparable jobs in the private sector. One calculation shows that GS–18s in the Senior Executive

---

11. Robert W. Hartman and Arnold R. Weber, *The Rewards of Public Service* (Brookings, 1980).

12. Grace, *War on Waste*, p. 236.

13. Sharon P. Smith, "Equal Pay in the Public Sector: Fact or Fantasy" (Department of Economics, Princeton University, 1977).

Table 1. *Percent Changes in Federal Civil Service Pay*[a]

	Federal pay increase	Pay agent recommendation	Consumer Price Index change
1971	5.96	5.96	4.3
1972	5.5	6.6	3.3
1973	4.77	4.77	6.2
1974	5.52	5.52	11.0
1975	5.0	8.66	9.1
1976	5.7	5.17	5.8
1977	7.05	7.05	6.5
1978	5.5	8.4	7.6
1979	7.0	10.38	11.5
1980	9.1	12.69	13.5
1981	4.8	15.1	8.5
1982	4.0	17.1	6.1
1983[b]	4.0	21.5	3.5
1984[c]	3.5	18.3	. . .

Source: Advisory Committee on Federal Pay, *Report on the Fiscal Year 1985 Pay Increase* (Advisory Committee on Federal Pay, 1984).

a. Average across pay grades.
b. Put into effect January 1984.
c. Begins January 1, 1985; annual rate is 2.6 percent.

Service earn approximately $30,000 less than they would earn in comparable positions in the private sector.[14] In real terms, a GS–18 earned almost 50 percent less in 1984 than he or she did in 1970.

The rather severe lagging of pay for senior civil servants happens largely because of the legislated relationship of civil service jobs to the pay of congressional representatives and political executives (the executive schedule). At present, a civil servant can earn no more than an E–V (an E–IV in the Senior Executive Service). The executive schedule is linked to congressional pay, so that an E–II can earn no more than a representative and, of course, an E–V must earn less than an E–II.[15] So, as Congress has raised its own pay slowly (although not its expense allowances) because of political pressure, and as the pay of lower echelon civil servants has moved upward, a significant pay compression in the senior ranks of the civil service has occurred. Often, employees in various steps and grades earn the same amount regardless of their nominal salaries as expressed in comparability tables. Performance bonuses

14. Advisory Committee on Federal Pay, *Report on the Fiscal 1984 Pay Increase Under the Federal Statutory Pay Systems* (Washington, D.C.: Advisory Committee on Federal Pay, 1983), table 3.

15. There are some instances in which civil servants do make more than their nominal political masters. This would be true of SES members earning bonuses and professionals such as physicians who are on special pay schemes.

for the Senior Executive Service were devised to compensate for lower salaries, but the bonuses have not been funded at the level originally intended. Rather naturally, the pay compression impairs the morale of many senior career executives in the federal service who can expect to gain little economically by continued service. What they can hope to gain is some increase in pension benefits, although those benefits are also under attack. These economic threats to senior career civil servants, as well as the resultant poor morale of the service, present the prospect of a serious "brain drain" from the civil service. A small number of senior civil servants will move into private sector positions; more will retire while the system remains as generous as it currently is. The Grace Commission notes that 508 career executives retired in 1977, but 3,137 retired in 1980. However, the average retirement age in the federal civil service (60.7 years in 1982) is only slightly lower than that in the private sector (61.8 years).

The perquisites of civil servants have been under both indirect and direct attacks. The direct attacks by the Grace Commission will be discussed next, but the indirect assaults have already had some effect. In making his 1983 recommendations on federal pay, President Ronald Reagan argued that the appropriate comparability figure for federal pay is not 100 percent of the average in the private sector, but 94 percent; the missing 6 percent covers benefits such as the index-linked pension and the relative security of the job. Others have suggested that civil servants should increase contributions to their pension programs to make the programs more actuarially sound.

Again, controversy about these issues is not limited to the United States. Civil service pay is also an important political issue—at least for the civil servants—in the United Kingdom and has been for some time. Since 1955 a comparability exercise (the Priestly system) similar to that used in the United States, and subject to similar problems in data collection, has offered recommendations for civil service pay. After Britain's civil service unions and Treasury had agreed upon the findings of the comparability exercise, the recommendations were usually implemented, except for some suspensions during periods of incomes policies.[16] In Britain, unions have been directly involved in the review and analysis of the comparability data, in contrast to the

16. P. B. Beaumont and J. W. Leopold, "Public Sector Industrial Relations in Britain: An Overview," *Public Administration Bulletin,* vol. 6 (Winter 1983), pp. 2–39.

more independent U.S. calculations of the president's pay agent and the Advisory Committee on Federal Pay.[17]

Britain's system of pay determination broke down almost entirely in 1979 when the government used the cash limit imposed upon public expenditure to override the recommendations of the pay research unit.[18] That event eventually led to the government's abrogation of the pay agreement with its unions. Pay was then set by free, collective bargaining within the cash limits that the government determined before opening negotiations with the unions. Rather naturally, the unions believe that the cash limit and the generally poor economic state of the country place most of the high cards in the deck in the hand of the government. In fact, by most estimates, public sector pay in Britain is now substantially below that in the private sector; one means of calculating the difference puts the figure at approximately 13 percent behind private sector pay, and in 1984 the independent Office of Manpower Economics recommended civil service raises of 7 percent in contrast to the 3.5 percent offered by the government.[19]

Some negotiators have attempted to revive a system of pay determination in the United Kingdom, based on the report of the Megaw Commission on Public Sector Pay.[20] The Megaw Commission proposed that bargaining between the unions and the government be carried on within the interquartile ranges of pay movements (increases) for three out of four years, with a full comparability survey to be carried out every fourth year. Thus in most years, civil servants could receive raises of at least slightly more than the lowest 25 percent of all raises in the country but less than the top 25 percent. The Megaw Commission also advocated comparing jobs on the basis of factors used to evaluate jobs rather than whole job comparison. In large part because of the charged political climate between organized public employees and the current government, the Megaw proposals have not been

17. One of the sticking points in the current negotiations over public sector pay is access for the unions to the raw data that would be used to calculate comparability recommendations.

18. Gwyn Bevan, Keith Sisson, and Philip Way, "Cash Limits and the Public Sector," *Public Administration,* vol. 59 (Winter 1981), p. 393.

19. Council of Civil Service Unions, *Your Vote Counts*; and *The Bulletin of the Council of Civil Service Unions* (London: Council of Civil Service Unions, May 1983 and April 1984, respectively).

20. Megaw Commission on Public Sector Pay, *Inquiry into Civil Service Pay*, Cmnd. 8590 (London: Her Majesty's Stationery Office, 1982).

implemented, and wages are still determined by bargaining within the constraints of the cash limit. The government and the unions are also far apart on the process of transition between the status quo and a new system. The government does not want to make up the current pay gap before implementing the Megaw system, and the unions quite naturally believe that would be essential to make the system acceptable to their members. Given its inclinations and the state of the British economy, the Thatcher government appears content to negotiate with its civil servants without a mutually agreed upon system of pay determination.

Interestingly, however, in the midst of this discussion about public sector pay the very top civil servants in Britain have maintained the comparability of their own pay levels with those in the private sector. Pay in the upper echelons of the civil service is covered by a separate Top Salaries Review Board, which has continued to suggest adjustments in the pay of the top three grades of the civil service. And, unlike those in the United States, senior civil servants in Britain earn more than the ministers whom they serve. Permanent secretaries as of this year make £42,750, while ministers earn £40,930. Even the prime minister earns less than the secretary to the cabinet. Although compensation has remained at or above private sector levels at the top of the scale, the British civil service has had difficulty in attracting young university graduates into the beginning grades of the executive group—not a brain drain but certainly a growing brain gap.[21] In both the United States and the United Kingdom, pay for public officials is an important political symbol, and keeping public sector wages low is a potent political weapon.

Weakening the Traditional Personnel Management System

At the same time that the comparability of reward for working within the public service has been eroding, other aspects of the personnel system have been changing, and changing in ways that do not benefit most civil servants. The basic pressure on the civil service system is to make it less of a monolithic system and more of a loosely related set of different groups of people working for the federal government. Such diversity might have certain advantages, but it would certainly eliminate the system's (relative) clarity and uniformity. Less uniformity might generate more internal controversies if one group or another perceives itself as disadvantaged by the absence of uniformity in pay.

21. David Walker, "Civil Service's Top Jobs Empty 'Because of Low Pay'," *New York Times*, April 24, 1984.

One way of breaking down the uniformity of the civil service system is to base pay for civil service positions on prevailing wages in local labor markets rather than on national averages and uniformity. The same wage for a position that might be below market rates in New York or San Francisco might be well above market rates in Hard Scrabble, Virginia. This would, of course, mean that civil service employees would be potentially of lower quality in major metropolitan areas but overpaid in lower cost markets. Furthermore, this could adversely affect mobility within the service, especially for midcareer officials, whose pay and perquisites tend to be more directly comparable to those in the private sector.

Government has begun to address the problem of payment for employees who could earn higher salaries in the private sector than in the public sector. For example, under the Physician's Comparability Act physicians can earn salaries more comparable to what they would earn in the private sector and therefore much higher than most civil servants' salaries. Also, for more than a decade the federal government has hired employees on a special rate basis, reflecting the higher wages paid for occupations such as engineers and technicians than would be available through the general schedule. As of 1984 about 34,000 employees were paid on this basis.[22] Recent attempts by the Office of Personnel Management to reduce the pay differentials of these employees by not granting them the raises granted to the rest of the civil service work force have resulted in losses of personnel and difficulties in recruitment. For many employees with professional and technical qualifications the nominal grading of their occupations may be increasingly meaningless as the need to "overgrade" the positions to be competitive with the private sector increases. In short, personnel managers favor changes in the general schedule system and its limited number of pay grades.

On the other side of the Atlantic the opposite move is taking place. The current public sector pay system in the United Kingdom has several hundred different occupational definitions, for example, dog handler and paper keeper, each with a different set of pay levels. The changes in the pay system recommended by the Megaw report would include development of pay bands similar to those in the general schedule system in the United States. Occupations would be placed into those bands by a system of job

22. Mike Causey, "GAO: U.S. Pay Lags for Hard-to-Get Workers," *Washington Post*, April 19, 1984.

evaluation such as the Hay system.[23] The civil service unions oppose this move. They fear that such a system would be too easily manipulated by the government and would break down the internal gradings among civil service jobs that have taken so long to devise.

Furthermore, the traditional definition of "merit" within the civil service is being attacked in several ways. For instance, under pressure from minority groups and the courts, the previously used examination for entry level clerical positions (PACE) within the civil service was first suspended by a consent decree under the Carter administration and then eliminated by the Reagan administration.[24] Although the suspension and subsequent elimination were initiated by a desire to make the system more equitable for those who may have been disadvantaged by the testing procedures, this change inevitably raises questions about the possible return to political favoritism in the allocation of these positions. Alan K. Campbell, director of the Office of Personnel Management in the Carter administration, argued that the abolition of the entry level test raised the possibility of a "movement away from objective selection . . . to other kinds of qualifications—ranging from political nepotism to random selection."[25] Such a return to the spoils system has not necessarily occurred because of the abolition of the PACE, but the potential exists for such an outcome.

The attempts to implement merit pay as a component of civil service reform are perceived by some as a move away from the merit principle and toward a reward system emphasizing attributes such as personal loyalty and political acceptability. Given the difficulties of measuring performance in many white-collar jobs in the federal government, those attempting to implement merit pay leave themselves open to the charge of personal or political bias. The traditional system of pay by grade and longevity certainly has its difficulties as a mechanism for managing personnel, but the substitution of another system in the context of the career civil service may present even greater difficulties.

Similar questions have been raised about how reductions in force have been implemented. One political question concerns reductions in force as a means of attacking services and programs

23. Megaw Commission, *Inquiry into Civil Service Pay*, pp. 138–46.

24. Sar A. Levitan and Alexandra B. Noden, *Working for the Sovereign* (Johns Hopkins University Press, 1983), pp. 111–13.

25. Quoted in Mike Causey, "PACE Is Abolished to Correct Its Bias," *Washington Post*, May 12, 1982.

that are unpopular with the Reagan administration. The more subtle mechanism by which merit system protections may be eroded is through the complex procedures for deciding the "competitive area" in which personnel may be bumped when a reduction in force is imposed.[26] Finally, the ability of a superior to rate an employee as "outstanding" on a performance appraisal prior to a reduction in force, which is the equivalent of four more years of seniority on a retention register, opens the way to the same types of personal and political favoritism that are present with awards of merit pay. In short, aside from the necessity or desirability of reducing employment in the federal government, the current procedures for conducting reductions in force are cumbersome, disruptive, and inefficient.[27]

Finally, the issue of comparable worth in federal employment is of increasing concern both to women's groups and to federal managers. Substantial evidence demonstrates that occupations, for example, nursing or secretarial positions, that traditionally have been dominated by women tend to be paid less than occupations dominated by men, although the positions require the same levels of skill.[28] Thus a whole new dimension to the issue of merit pay arises and poses the possibility of a large increase in the bill for the federal government if the advocates of comparable worth are successful.

Politicizing the Civil Service

Another important trend in contemporary civil service politics in Washington is the apparently increasing politicization and unionization of the federal work force. The attacks on the merit system indicate the trend toward politicization, but other forces are at work as well.

One could make the argument that to some degree the civil service has been highly politicized and has been politicized in a direction favoring Democratic party issues.[29] The great expansions

26. Levitan and Noden, *Working for the Sovereign*, p. 119.

27. Karlyn Baker, " 'Reagan Roulette' and Its Impact" *Washington Post*, February 28, 1982.

28. Steven A. Neuse, "A Critical Perspective on the Comparable Worth Debate," *Review of Public Personnel Administration*, vol. 3, no. 1 (1982), pp. 1–20; E. R. Livernash, ed., *Comparable Worth: Issues and Alternatives* (Washington, D.C.: Equal Employment Advisory Council, 1980); for similar issues in the United Kingdom, see P. B. Beaumont, *Government as Employer—Setting an Example?* (London: Royal Institute of Public Administration, 1981).

29. See Bert A. Rockman, "Bureaucracy, Power and Policy: The State of the Field," paper presented at the 1984 annual meeting of the American Political Science Association, p. 31.

of the federal civil service occurred during the New Deal and the Great Society eras so that many of the people in social service, environmental, labor, and similar organizations in government would have been recruited under Democratic administrations and could be expected to have some commitments to the programs of the Democratic party. Any Republican president who does not share a commitment to those programs will have some difficulty in making civil servants the neutral executors of the will of the people. Thus attempts of the current administration to place more decisionmaking power in the central agencies such as the Office of Management and Budget, the Office of Personnel Management, and the Executive Office of the President, and to place more tiers of political appointees on top of career officials in many departments, may be seen as a natural reaction to a group of civil servants perceived as hostile to its programs.

The president now has much greater authority over senior civil servants because of the Civil Service Reform Act of 1978 and the formation of the Senior Executive Service—Carter's gift to Reagan. The SES was probably intended as a neutral management tool that would allow for a more efficient and effective civil service—much as merit pay was conceived. But the ability of personnel managers to dismiss senior civil servants in the SES, to reassign them to less sensitive positions, and to reward those whom they deem to have performed in an outstanding manner allows much greater political control over the career service than was ever true previously.[30] The SES members were also given more options for taking political jobs in an administration. Consequently, some executives may well be forced to resign from the public service when there is a change in administration. The Reagan administration has further politicized the SES by placing all general SES jobs in the "plum book" following the 1984 election, making those jobs available to political appointees.

Again, many of these trends appear in the United Kingdom, although the discussion of the possibility of a committed civil service has been somewhat more public. Sir John Hoskyns, Mrs. Thatcher's former chief adviser, argued that a "radical government" may also need a radically minded civil service.[31] Besides

30. See, for example, Peter W. Colby and Patricia W. Ingraham, "Civil Service Reform: The Views of the Senior Executive Service," paper presented at the 1981 annual meeting of the American Society for Public Administration; and Patricia W. Ingraham and Carolyn Ban, eds., *Legislating Bureaucratic Change* (SUNY, 1984).

31. Sir John Hoskyns, "Whitehall and Westminster: An Outsider's View," *Fiscal Studies,* vol. 3 (Nov. 3, 1982), pp. 162–72.

mere argument, certain actions taken can be interpreted as polit-
icizing the civil service. In one instance, Mrs. Thatcher has
intervened in the appointment of senior civil servants—permanent
secretaries in particular—more than most previous prime ministers. This has resulted in the appointment of several very young
permanent secretaries in key positions.[32] It has been generally
assumed that she picked these civil servants because of their style
rather than their politics; she is known to abhor the traditional
obsequious and chameleonlike civil service style. In any case, the
appearance of partisan intervention may be as important as the
reality. Civil servants so appointed may find it difficult to
effectively serve a Labour government—especially a Labour government that may be committed to radical changes. In addition,
critics of the British policymaking system have publicly demanded
a civil service system that includes political executives who come
and go with governments—much like the American system of
political executives. This change would politicize a number of
key positions now held by permanent civil servants.

While the senior portions of the American civil service have
become politicized in a partisan manner, the American civil service
as a whole has become politicized to protect its own pay and
position. The general decline in pay and conditions of employment
mentioned, as well as ideological attacks on the civil service, has
led to an increased membership of civil servants in unions and
other labor organizations. In 1982 approximately 61 percent of all
federal employees (86 percent of the blue-collar work force and
54 percent of the white-collar work force) were members of labor
unions (this figure does not include members of professional
organizations that may at times function as labor unions). And as
the strikers in the Professional Air Traffic Controllers Organization
revealed, at least some portions of the unionized work force have
been willing to press their demands to an extent not thought
possible previously. The crushing defeat of the organization will
give any future federal strikers cause for alarm, but it is not at all
clear that the federal work force will ever again be as quiescent
as it once was. The general change in the position of the civil
service and the need to organize to protect pay and perquisites
resulted in a confrontational mentality between the civil service
work force and its management. Previously, organizations such
as the Civil Service League could serve as mediators in any disputes

32. F. F. Ridley, "The British Civil Service and Politics: Principles in Question and
Traditions in Flux," *Parliamentary Affairs,* vol. 36 (Winter, 1983), pp. 28–48.

between government as employer and the civil service work force; now, little restrains the rhetoric of labor relations in government from being like that in the soft coal industry.

In the United Kingdom, where the government is at least indirectly the soft coal industry, the confrontational style has existed between government and some of its employees for some time. What is new is the spread of union militancy to white-collar employees and even to senior white-collar employees. The transformation of the First Division Association from an association of the very top officials of the civil service into a virtual trade union, now affiliated with the Trade Union Congress, has been especially notable. The British government's decision to ban union membership for the staff of the government communications headquarters, a major defense facility, has accentuated the militancy of white-collar unions. The decision was made on the grounds of security, but it has deeply angered the unions and united them against the government, at least on this one issue.

Finally, the American civil service becomes increasingly politicized as it seeks to enlist the support of Congress in its fight for improved wages. The federal civil service has now become a political actor and is increasingly willing to use its political strengths, both as organized workers and as a large block of voters, to press demands for better pay and working conditions. Thus any politician who seeks to impose unwanted changes on the civil service will not find that task as easy now as it has been in the past.

The Grace Commission

The President's Private Sector Survey on Cost Control (the Grace Commission) submitted a report in January 1984 recommending changes in the federal civil service, particularly affecting its management. Some proposals are not radically new; for example, contracting out of federal jobs has been discussed, advocated, and to some degree implemented by the past several presidents. Some of the proposals are radical, recommending changes in the treatment of federal workers that might significantly affect the morale and retention of workers. The proposals seem to be based on a set of assumptions, rather widely held in the business community and perhaps in the population as a whole, about the federal work force.

The Bureaucracy Rampant

The most fundamental assumption implicit in the Grace Commission report is that the federal bureaucracy is rampant and is

Table 2. *Federal Civilian Employment as a Percent of the Labor Force*

	Federal civilian employment as percent of labor force	Federal civilian employment as percent of total employment
1984	2.56	2.78
1983	2.53	2.82
1982	2.60	2.88
1981	2.67	2.87
1980	3.10	3.33
1975	3.13	3.42
1970	3.49	3.72
1965	3.44	3.64
1960	3.43	3.66

Source: *Statistical Abstract of the United States, 1983* (Government Printing Office, 1984); and B. Guy Peters, "Public Employment in the United States," in R. Rose and others, *Public Employment in Western Democracies* (Cambridge University Press, forthcoming).

by now too large. That assumption should be examined by analyzing the size of the federal government in relation to a particular standard. Few if any objective standards for comparison exist. Compared with its historical size, the federal bureaucracy is not particularly large at present and was not so even before the beginning of the Reagan administration and the round of reductions imposed on the civil service. Table 2 shows the size of the federal civil service for several decades in relation to the entire labor force. Clearly, the civil service has declined as a proportion of the labor force, and in the Reagan years the nondefense civilian work force has declined especially rapidly. In other words, the size of the federal work force has not kept pace with demographic growth in the United States. There is no particular reason that the civil service should have remained a constant or growing percentage of the labor force; automation and fixed needs for certain types of work (only one person is needed as director of an agency regardless of how many people there are in the country) could obviate the need for more civil servants. But clearly a rapid expansion of the federal work force has not occurred.

Civil service compensation has not been growing in relationship to the economy as a whole. Total civil service wages and salaries as a percentage of all wages and salaries paid in the economy have been declining, as could be surmised by the declining relative size of the civil service and the declining relative wages of civil servants (table 2). The federal work force is large, and many of its members are well paid, and some may well be overpaid. But the federal work force is not a Leviathan attempting to take over the government and economy—at least not on the basis of these data.

Pensions and Retirement

A principal contention of the Grace Commission is that the civil service and military retirement systems are more generous than those in the private sector and are excessively generous. The commission cited the early age at which civil servants can retire with full benefits and the cost-of-living adjustments built into public sector pensions that are available in very few private sector plans. While the evidence about the relative generosity of private and public sector benefit packages is somewhat shaky and open to interpretation—the General Accounting Office, for example, found that the benefit package offered by the Grace Company itself is at least as good for some types of employees as that in the civil service—the current balance between pay while in work and pensions does pose important questions about managing the federal civil service.[33]

The first issue concerns the appropriate balance between pay while in work and pay after retirement. The current system— especially for top executives—appears to offer inadequate rewards for hard work, advancement, and remaining in office and provides every incentive to retire as soon as possible. This is especially true when the combination of pay compression and cost-of-living adjustments for pensions could mean that a person can receive as much or more while retired than if he or she stays on the job. The retirement system may be deferred compensation, but would it not be wiser to reward the civil servant while in office rather than later when no productive benefit can be gained from that reward?

Another important issue concerns just how to make changes. Many people have chosen a civil service career in part because of the pension program, or at least they were willing to accept the potentially lower current income in a civil service job in exchange for the security of an inflation-proofed pension in the future. How can a movement away from the current system be made without damaging, perhaps severely, those employees? The possible answers seem twofold. The first is to inflict the damages that might satisfy the goal of cutting costs even at a potentially high price in morale and efficiency. An alternative is to phase in changes in the pension program gradually with newly hired or recent employees.

33. U.S. General Accounting Office, "Comparison of Retirement Benefits for W. R. Grace and Company and Civil Service Employees" (GAO/OCG-84-1, June 12, 1984).

This approach would meet the goals of equity and fairness but would do little to reduce costs in the short run. Further, without reform of the pay system, cutting pensions could have potentially harmful effects on recruitment, especially the recruitment of managerial personnel.

Overgrading

The Grace Commission also questioned "overgrading." Overgrading is in quotation marks because it is not clear on what standard the grading of civil service positions is to be judged. The standard that the Grace Commission chose was the distribution of grades and salaries in private sector firms. So, for example, the commission found that 2.8 times as large a proportion of federal employees as private sector employees were employed in positions of GS–11 or its equivalent.[34] The obvious question is whether the private sector is the appropriate source of comparison. Some of the characteristics of work in the public sector, for example, the need to give more attention to equality and equity in making decisions, may force more managerial oversight than would be true in the private sector. Of course, even if that is true, the factor of 2.8 implies a great deal of oversight, and several studies have shown a substantial degree of misgrading of federal workers, especially in the GS–13 to GS–15 levels.[35] The more important question is whether work in the public sector can be organized in the same manner as work in the private sector.

The other point about overgrading, which the commission pointed out, is that overgrading may be a thinly disguised means of compensating for the deficiencies of entry level pay, especially for professional occupations such as engineers, accountants, and attorneys. Further, given that public programs are most commonly evaluated by total output rather than efficiency—assuming that either of those characteristics can be accurately measured in public programs—program managers have an incentive to hire at as high a level as possible. As long as the more qualified or higher graded employee can add more output to the organization than a lower graded employee, there is an incentive to hire at the higher level.[36]

34. Grace, *War on Waste*, pp. 233–36.
35. U.S. Civil Service Commission, Bureau of Personnel Management Evaluation, *A Report on the Study of Position Classification Accuracy in Executive Branch Occupations* (GPO, 1978).
36. Robert W. Hartman, *Pay and Pensions for Federal Workers* (Brookings, 1983), pp. 37–40.

Conclusions This essay has briefly described important changes that have been occurring in the federal civil service; changes that have been occurring in the civil service of the United Kingdom; and findings of the Grace Commission concerning personnel management in the federal government. From these descriptions I can draw three conclusions.

First, the Grace Commission and its recommendations, even if justified by the evidence, could hardly have come at a more inopportune time for the federal civil service. The report appears to be one more attack on the role of the civil service in American government and on the conditions of employment for individual civil servants. Certainly, things are wrong with personnel administration in the federal government—the poor pay of senior executives, overgrading of many positions, and difficulties in implementing the principles of a merit system—but the rather consistent string of attacks on the civil service, both rhetorical and against their checkbooks, is certain to hurt morale, recruitment, and retention. If the civil service continues to underpay senior executives and professionals, accepts reductions in other benefits, and continues to have its civil service protections whittled away, then the civil service may well become the mediocre and inefficient service that the stereotype so often portrays.

Second, the American case is by no means isolated. What is interesting is the development of a "Washminster mutation." The civil service systems and the relationship between civil servants and ministers in the United States and the United Kingdom are becoming more similar. This growing similarity is occurring on several fronts. Clearly, the size and presumed privileged position of the career civil service is a political issue in both countries. As one part of that issue, the pay of civil servants is an important concern in both countries. There have also been increasing political pressures on the civil service to be more committed to the programs of the current administrations. Finally, the civil service is a negative political symbol for many people on both sides of the Atlantic, and there is a great deal to be gained politically by running against the civil service. The use of the Grace Commission by President Reagan is one manifestation of that tendency. The real question is whether the recommendations, if adopted, would improve the nature of the service rendered to citizens or would merely worsen the lot of civil servants.

Finally, it is by no means clear that the private sector and private sector management are the most appropriate standards of comparison for public sector management. There is a long tradition—less long in Britain than in the United States—of assuming that a well-managed government would necessarily resemble a business. This assumption may be wrong for two reasons. First, government is different in many ways from the private sector, and demands for accountability, responsiveness, and equity are much greater in the public sector than in the private sector. This in turn may mean that there is more redundancy, more middle-level supervisors, and more paperwork. Second, many businesses, if forced to undergo the scrutiny that the public sector regularly undergoes, might be found to harbor many of the same inefficiencies found in government, or perhaps just different ones. The management of any large, complex organization is a difficult task, but government may be better understood as a large, complex, public organization rather than just another large organization.

General Discussion

DUNCAN BAILEY began the discussion by reiterating that the purpose of the conference was a search for the fundamental principles of personnel management. He said that the Grace Commission intended to draw upon the sound principles of business management and relate them to the federal government's personnel practices. Choosing to avoid a discussion of pensions, Bailey addressed pay comparability between the public and private sectors; the Senior Executive Service (SES); pay compression; and procedures for reductions in force. He restated the Grace Commission's findings that the federal government overpays blue-collar workers; the method of determining pay comparability for white-collar workers is flawed; the SES has been a failure, it should be cut in half and the remaining half should be given raises of about 25 percent; the link between federal executive pay and congressional pay should be severed; and current procedures for reductions in force lead to overgrading to protect employees.

Jerry Shaw, chairman of the Public Employees Roundtable and General Council of the Senior Executives Association, commented on the assertions in the Grace Commission report that federal employees are overpaid, that their benefits are too generous, and that nearly all the deficit problems in the country are the fault of federal employees. Shaw argued that the Grace Commission's personnel recommendations focus exclusively on how much money can be taken out of the federal employee's hide. He said that the changes in benefits recommended by the Grace Commission would reduce the quality and service delivery capacity of the government. Shaw addressed some specific recommendations, for example, the proposal to reduce the size of the SES and the proposal to include small private sector firms with as few as twenty-five employees in the pay comparability survey. He said that these changes would make the federal government a weak labor market competitor for professional and technical talent.

Malcom Lovell, a visiting guest scholar at Brookings and former under secretary of labor, commented that building and maintaining a splendid civil service, attracting the people that are capable of serving the country well, and maintaining reasonable

40

control over the cost of the service are central concerns. He said that the key to balancing the need for a competent civil service with cost controls lies in working out compromises between political interests.

Murray Comarow, distinguished adjunct professor in residence, the American University, and former executive director, President's Commission on Executive Organization (Ash Council), asked what standards of performance the government ought to use, since it does not have a profit criterion.

Bailey responded that the central issue is that the personnel principles that have been developed among private sector companies have been honed by hundreds of years of experience in a profit and loss environment. Such issues include what can be afforded in fringe benefits, raises, merit, and other conditions affecting employees. These kinds of principles ought to be applied to the personnel problems of the federal government.

Comarow said that he did not understand the relationship between longevity and excellence. Because businesses have been around for hundreds of years, it does not follow that their personnel principles are uniquely sound. Governments have also been around for hundreds of years. The incentives and disincentives are radically different in the government sector and the private sector.

Bailey responded that he believed the incentives in both sectors are similar. He also said that the surviving companies are profitable and that unlike the federal government, no company has ever managed to lose $170 billion in a single year.

Charles Goodsell, professor of public administration at Virginia Polytechnic Institute and State University, asked whether the Grace Commission's recommendations make good sense for either a corporation or the federal government and wondered how a good corporate manager would handle the morale problem in the federal government.

Bailey replied that a good corporate manager would cut the work force to the bone; the Grace Commission does not propose cutting to the bone, just cutting out the fat. Morale problems are something to be expected under the circumstances.

O. Glen Stahl, a scholar in the field of public personnel administration, identified several things in the Grace Commission report that he agreed with and would like to discuss further, for example, employee training, work force planning, and pay comparability. Stahl observed that the occupational makeup of the public and private sectors is very different. He also saw no assurance that the Grace Commission was motivated to insure that federal government service had a high caliber work force with high morale. Instead of just an average system, he thought that the federal government personnel system ought to be compared with the very best personnel systems in our whole economy.

Lovell asked whether the panel thought the civil service system is becoming less a merit system and more a system in which political and other influences are rampant.

Shaw responded that from the point of view of career executives and mid-level managers, the political changes in this country are fearsome. He said that even though there are good things in the Grace Commission report, the political climate makes discussion about them impossible. The administration is not willing to negotiate balanced changes that will lower some costs and change other things to produce a quality work force.

Patrick Korten, executive assistant director for policy and communications for the Office of Personnel Management, responded that anyone who knows Capitol Hill, knows that the public employee groups are the most powerful, single lobby in Washington. If there is something an employee group does not want done, chances are it will not be done. The Grace people are trying to overcome the political obstacles by generating public interest about an issue that is not very interesting to the average American. When that kind of diffuse interest competes with the precise and carefully focused attention of public employee groups, it is at a disadvantage.

Lovell remarked that there appeared to be more room for bargaining and packaging reforms than Korten might have heard.

Bailey brought the discussion back to the issue of making political appointments to the SES by remarking that he thought the SES should be kept separate from career appointees. He also responded to Stahl's comment about the lack of commitment to excellence for the federal service reflected in the commission's attitude. By using the top 200 or 300 largest firms as a model, he stated, the commission was using the very best as a standard.

Klepner asked B. Guy Peters how much collective bargaining plays a central role in Great Britain in determining levels of pay, retirement, and fringe benefits and whether such a system would work here.

Peters responded that for the most part collective bargaining is more important in the United Kingdom than in this country, although certain benefit and pension levels have been excluded from the process. Peters was reluctant to advocate full, open collective bargaining to resolve all the problems in the public sector. He stated that in Britain, it has produced as many problems as solutions.

The Grace Commission's Challenge to Public Personnel Administration

EUGENE B. McGREGOR, JR.

THE CURRENT DRIVE to improve government productivity has led to a scrutiny of the state of the art in public personnel administration. In fact, the issues raised by the President's Private Sector Survey on Cost Control (hereafter the Grace Commission) culminate in a redefinition of that art. Whether the commission's estimates were precise, whether the research was of uniform quality, or whether a 'private' business bias dominated the analysis is not the focus of attention. The compelling point is that within twenty-one months, a skilled group of managerial "outsiders" concluded that federal personnel management practice falls short of the current state of the art. After auditing federal personnel operations the commission asserted the following:

—Federal administration now incurs some unusual personnel costs in its packaging of wages, salaries, and fringe benefits.

—The government could take advantage of more cost-effective ways to design employment systems and manage federal personnel.

—Currently, governmentwide management of the federal work force does not exist, though some innovative management occurs in particular agencies and bureaus.

—The size of personnel costs and the savings possible with effective work force management justify a careful scrutiny of federal personnel practices.

This essay assesses the commission's definition of effective human resource management and its application to federal practice. Many improvements have occurred recently in federal personnel operations in job analysis and evaluation; pay and performance management; the use of computerized forecasting and planning models; and the development of human resource information systems.[1] But operations management is not the main problem

1. *Report of the Job Evaluation and Pay Review Task Force to the United States Civil Service Commission,* prepared for the Subcommittee on Employee Benefits of the House Committee on Post Office and Civil Service, 92 Cong. 2 sess. (Government Printing Office, 1972); U.S. Department of Health and Human Services, *Performance Planning Review and Appraisal*

that the commission found in federal personnel management. The main problem is managing the work force.

For the most part, personnel operations comprise the policies, procedures, and technical routines used to recruit, select, train, appraise, compensate, develop, and discipline a labor force. Thus personnel operation has been largely concerned with "supply-side" issues that determine the availability of personnel for public service, and an extensive scholarly literature catalogues the practices of personnel offices.[2] Consequently, a preponderance of personnel scholarship covers questions traditionally associated with an auxiliary staff function. The research has not been unproductive. On the contrary, it documents an extraordinary diversity of ways to conduct personnel operations. Indeed, a quick review of the standard personnel management journals reveals numerous personnel management techniques and an explosion in the production of supporting computer software for human resource information systems (HRIS) and computerized decision support systems.[3]

State-of-the-art operations technique does not necessarily advance work force management for several reasons. For one thing, state-of-the-art operations can take a variety of technical forms. In this respect both public and private sectors have made enormous strides and have much to share. But technical sophistication is not to be confused with management. The public management challenge is to determine which of the available techniques best suits the goals and objectives of public organizations. A second distinction is that human resource management in the public sector depends on a determination of personnel requirements. These requirements are based on public policy. Policy issues, in turn, require answers to such questions as the relationship between the government work force and the rest of the political economy; the

Guide: Model System (GPO, 1979); Harry L. Clark and Dona R. Thurston, *Planning Your Staffing Needs: A Handbook for Personnel Workers,* U.S. Civil Service Commission, Bureau of Policies and Standards (GPO, 1977); and U.S. Department of State, *Human Resources Information Systems for the U.S. Department of State* (GPO, 1977).

2. Major personnel administration journals and magazines include the following (available founding dates and sponsoring organizations are in parentheses): *Personnel* (American Management Association, 1923); *Personnel Journal* (1921); *Personnel Psychology* (1947); *Personnel Administration* (American Society for Personnel Administration, 1955); *Personnel Management* (Institute for Personnel Management, United Kingdom, 1968); *Public Personnel Management* (International Personnel Management, 1971); and *Compensation Administration.*

3. Barbara E. Heiken and James W. Randell, Jr., "Customizing Software for Human Resources," *Personnel Administrator,* vol. 29 (August 1984), pp. 43–48.

design and evaluation of public sector employment systems; the resources available for direct government employment; and the productivity of the public work force. A quick operations fix, such as a salary survey, a human resource information system, a manpower planning model, or a new performance appraisal system, will not resolve such issues.

A final disparity between operations and management is that operations-based discussions tend to focus on the details such as staffing, performance appraisal, compensation administration, career development, and employee relations. A discussion of how to match people and productivity requirements is often absent. Yet the design and selection of options for equating personnel requirements and availability defines the management agenda.

The Grace Commission report avoids focusing on operational detail. Instead, the report fixes attention on the key weakness in an otherwise sophisticated system of federal personnel administration.[4] It is that governmentwide work force management does not exist. The federal system does not currently have a way of determining the strategic work force requirements of government and managing the skill mix and staffing levels needed to deliver the final products and services mandated by public policy.

In one sense, work force requirements and personnel availability are an identity, and over time the effective personnel demand and supply will be equal. The management problem is to construct the balance on terms compatible with the goals and objectives of public policy. Thus an intermediate conclusion seems justified that the challenge in personnel administration is not a matter of achieving a higher operational sophistication. The real challenge entails linking personnel operations and strategic management.[5] The paucity of literature on the subject emphasizes that much remains to be done.[6]

The Grace Commission's insight

The Grace Commission clearly understood the strategic issues separating work force management from personnel operations.[7] Its conclusions, however, are deceptive, for they appear to be

4. President's Private Sector Survey on Cost Control, J Peter Grace, chairman, *War on Waste* (Macmillan, 1984). (Hereafter Grace, *War on Waste*).

5. Noel M. Tichy, Charles L. Fombrun, and Mary Anne Devanna, "Strategic Human Resource Management," *Sloan Management Review,* vol. 23 (Winter 1982), pp. 47–61.

6. Journals that appear to be most closely aligned with problems of work force management include recent issues of *Human Systems Management* (1980), and *Human Resource Management* (1961).

7. Grace, *War on Waste,* pp. 228–302.

standard pleas for eliminating waste. For instance, the commission suggested reducing payroll costs by introducing true comparability into federal wage and salary, retirement, and fringe benefit packages. It advocated the elimination of overstaffing and over-grading managerial positions. It urged the use of incentives for productivity improvement, and it advised eliminating unnecessary overtime pay and payroll padding with temporary positions.

Such suggestions are the standard "volume up, costs down" recommendations that public managers expect from the business community. The efficiency plea is perennial and necessary but insufficient for operations as complex as the federal government. Indeed, most productivity improvement reports that apply simple efficiency solutions to complex organizational problems are as unreliable for private business as they are for public bureaus and agencies.[8]

The Grace Commission went beyond simple efficiency analysis, however. The real question for this presidential commission was whether large scale inefficiency and waste could be documented and whether projected savings from personnel management improvement could retrieve a measurable share of the federal deficit. Since presidential attention is not ordinarily fixed on fine details such as retirement systems, fringe benefit packages, and personnel planning, the commission quite understandably attached the biggest numbers it could to attract the attention of public policymakers, usually bored by small budget numbers. Thus plans to retrieve $91 billion of a three-year $424 billion cost reduction program can at least be credited with getting public attention at a time when large deficits loom.

How are public management insiders to respond to an external review by private management outsiders who conclude that over a three-year period more than $400 billion in waste can be wrung out of government operations? (Twenty-one percent of that figure is attributed to flawed government personnel management.) Two responses can occur. One is discrediting the commission and its findings. That can be done by raising questions about the applicability, precision, and accuracy of the findings. The option is tempting because the report is clearly vulnerable.[9] Another re-

8. Arnold S. Judson, "The Awkward Truth about Productivity," *Harvard Business Review,* vol. 60 (September–October 1982), pp. 93–97.

9. U.S. Congressional Budget Office and U.S. General Accounting Office, *Analysis of the Grace Commission's Major Proposals for Cost Control* (GPO, 1984); *Report of the Task Force on Personnel Management of the President's Private Sector Survey on Cost Control,* Hearing before the Subcommittee on Investigations of the House Committee on Post Office and

sponse is discounting the value of the recommendations by the extent to which improvements in efficiency depend on changes in public policy that would require the unlikely cooperation of Congress. Then, career public managers can hide in the intricacies of the policy process and ignore the substance of the report.

Another option, however, is to consider the report, bearing in mind the constraints placed on the commission. The speed with which 2,000 volunteers, organized into thirty-six task force groups, assembled over 2,500 recommendations in 750 issue areas, and—between March 1982 and January 1984—drafted a forty-nine volume blueprint for public management action is striking. Clearly, this report was not an exercise in scholarly analysis, and it should surprise no one that the report concurred with the commission's initial assumption that improving personnel management can lead to a reduction in the budget deficit.

Most important, as stated previously, the commission has stressed the absence of an active, governmentwide management of the federal work force. The opening paragraph of the personnel report makes the point.

> Work force management determines the number of people and skills necessary to accomplish an organization's objectives, and the actions necessary to obtain, develop, and motivate the work force. Work force requirements, however, have received little attention in Government because budget decisions are usually overriding, there is lack of leadership from the Office of Personnel Management (OPM), and there is insufficient information to develop complete and integrated management systems. As a result, there is a need for human resource planning procedures that would allow for uniform decision making throughout the Federal Government regarding the size, composition, allocation, and development of work force needs.[10]

The finding is strategic for all recommendations in the commission's personnel report. In effect, the commission finds that the federal government is attempting to manage a large and expensive work force by using only the leverage that accrues to the Office of Personnel Management's control of personnel operations and the Office of Management and Budget's allocations of cost, average grade, and employment ceilings. Furthermore, the civilian personnel system is run by a central agency—the Office of Personnel Management (OPM)—whose stock-in-trade

Civil Service, 98 Cong. 1 sess. (GPO, 1983); and Charles T. Goodsell, "The Grace Commission: Seeking Efficiency for the Whole People?" *Public Administration Review,* no. 3 (May–June 1984), pp. 196–204.

10. Grace, *War on Waste,* pp. 228–29.

historically has been limited to operations management. The OPM is not small. Its operating budget of $157 million and a work force of about 5,000 employees achieve a staffing standard of roughly 0.24 full-time equivalent (f.t.e.) administrative staff per 100 federal employees (roughly 1 OPM employee per 420 federal workers). In effect, if one accepts an industrial personnel staffing standard of 0.7 to 1.0 f.t.e. personnel staff per 100 employees as reasonable for a public sector personnel service, then the OPM claims 24 to 34 percent of the industrial standard without including personnel specialists assigned to the line departments, bureaus, and agencies.[11]

The key point is not an implied allegation of OPM overstaffing. The mission of the OPM is complex and includes a big investment in security investigations. Thus the portfolio of the federal OPM is not directly comparable with the portfolio of responsibilities managed by a private sector personnel office. The point is that public managers have no human resource management system for a work force of 2.1 million nonpostal civilians that costs $51 billion annually in direct wages and salaries and $41.7 billion in fringe benefit costs connected with retirement, health benefits, and life insurance. Missing, or at least obscure to the Grace Commission and everyone with whom task force members talked, is the formulation of federal personnel operating requirements. Yet requirements determine the adequacy of on-board staffing and the level of staffing need.[12]

The commission also discovered that no information system to support a managerial examination of the federal work force is in place. Such a system would establish the link between the final products of government and the role of personnel in complex systems of production. An information system helpful to managerial decisionmaking would classify the work force according to its contribution to productivity, its cost, and its chief characteristics compared with the competitive alternatives. Current government information systems do not produce such data. Current government personnel information systems collect, store, and generate reports about personnel biodata, performance appraisals, payroll status and costs, the characteristics of an applicant pool, and

11. Ibid., pp. 251–52.
12. In this analysis, staffing needs means the staffing actions necessary to equate requirements and availability. The formulation of requirements, availability, and needs is slightly different from published government statements, Clark and Thurston, *Planning Your Staffing Needs;* but it appears to follow a generally acceptable logic. See also James W. Walker, *Human Resource Planning* (McGraw-Hill, 1980).

employment histories of on-board or recently employed personnel.[13] Thus most government personnel information systems are designed with personnel operations, not executive-level management, in mind.

The failure to establish a productivity link between governmental human resource operations and information systems means that many important questions about federal personnel simply cannot be answered. In some cases, the system may fool itself. For instance, the Grace Commission charges that the federal work force is overgraded, underproductive, and overpaid compared with private sector counterparts. Thus staffing comparisons were adduced that showed the upward movement in average grade levels, the 'overstaffing' of management positions, the flaws in the pay comparability survey, and the gap between higher federal wage grade rates and lower prevailing local wages. The absence of productivity measurement systems that would justify the alleged comparative financial advantages enjoyed by federal workers was also documented.

What conclusion can be drawn? The Grace Commission concluded that federal personnel practices should be pulled into line with 'more efficient' private practice. The conclusion is both plausible and forceful. Only the executive levels of the federal work force were deemed systematically underpaid and, even then, the issue is the compensation owed to true public executives as opposed to highly graded employees whose positions simply converted to Senior Executive Service (SES) status with the passage of the Civil Service Reform Act of 1978. The attrition rates at the SES level of government do indeed suggest that an inadequate set of rewards results in the loss of executives crucial to the operation of the federal government. The absence of attrition at lower levels of the white-collar service suggests that the rewards there are more than adequate. Furthermore, it is entirely proper to compare federal personnel systems with work forces found in private firms, state and local government, not-for-profit corporations, and public authorities and corporations. Those entities are actual or potential federal instrumentalities, and they compete for federal work. The implication of such comparison is clear. If it is true that the federal work force is excessively layered, overstaffed in highly graded positions, and overpaid compared with nonfederal work forces performing similar work, corrections should be made. Without internal improvements in federal personnel practice, the work

13. Heiken and Randell, "Customizing Software for Human Resources," pp. 43–48.

load can be moved to other parts of the economy at enormous potential public savings.

There is, however, another possibility. It is that federal grading, staffing, and pay have changed to reflect changing federal goals and responsibilities. Consequently, an increasingly sophisticated work force must be graded and paid at levels exceeding nominal private sector rates. This is a requirements-side response to the commission's supply-side generalizations. The argument is speculative, yet some evidence exists that massive changes in the federal skill mix have occurred since World War II.[14] It also seems plausible that many changes in the federal work force are driven by the federal role at the cutting edge of a highly advanced postindustrial economy. Science, technology, and knowledge management increasingly characterize the federal mission along with bureaucratic and production management responsibilities. This line of argument implies that much federal work is really unlike much of the nonfederal economy and that federal productivity standards and work requirements demand a staffing structure, a skill mix, and a compensation package necessary to attract and retain a highly trained professional work force. In other words, the Grace Commission could be dead wrong in its assessment of the structure and management of the federal work force.

Which position is correct? The significance of the commission's personnel report is its finding that "nobody knows."[15] Neither the commission nor its critics can document allegations about the strategic basis for federal personnel practice. There is no solid information base that documents the human resource requirements of federal work and compares the requirements with on-board availability. There is no validated cross-walk that permits a direct comparison of federal and nonfederal work forces. The salary survey is too narrow to be useful for comparative analytic purposes. The commission was not even able to penetrate the aggregate computation of average grade to realize what a 61.5 percent average grade increase from 1949 to 1981 might conceivably mean. For instance, the report is oblivious to the fact that over the thirty-two-year span under review, federal operations have changed enormously, and personnel requirements were not left untouched. After all, the rise of the research and development

14. Frederick C. Mosher, *Democracy and Public Service* (Oxford University Press, 1968); Arthur J. Gartaganis, "Trends in Federal Employment," *Monthly Labor Review,* vol. 97 (October 1974), pp. 17–25.

15. Grace, *War on Waste,* p. 232.

agencies, the growth of computerized entitlement programs, and the vast contracting of federal missions to remote instrumentalities requires a vastly more sophisticated and professional work force than that required by a simpler and smaller federal mission. In short, a detailed factual basis for the conclusions of the Grace Commission cannot be found.

That, however, is the key insight of the commission. What the Grace Commission has documented is the extent of the federal government's ignorance about its own operation! The commission could not be more discriminating in its analysis of federal personnel management because federal managers themselves do not have the data that would demonstrate the adequacy or inadequacy of their own practices.

Government productivity

The commission's insight leads to another question and line of discussion about the state of the public personnel art. If the data on the federal work force will not sustain a managerial investigation of its structure and management, why not? The full answer would derail discussion of the main thesis, but one brief answer is that there is not a central management office in government that wants to know the answers to questions about how to convert the program goals of government into staffing requirements in order to adequately staff operating bureaus. The two obvious candidates—the OPM and the OMB—have traditionally dealt with staff services associated, respectively, with personnel operations and budget examination. The most active agency currently pressing a genuine managerial agenda on the executive branch is the General Accounting Office (GAO); yet, the GAO is in the wrong institutional position to design and operate a system for federal human resource management. Thus except for the occasional presidential query that generates an awkward White House foray into civil service management, there appears to be no institutional interest in governmentwide examination of the federal work force.

The result is unfortunate. Without publicly defended analyses of federal operating requirements, the whole system is vulnerable to perennial suspicions that too much is being spent on the wrong kinds of employees. The temptation is irresistible to apply some standard—any standard—to governmental work forces to estimate the real federal staffing requirements. Without any suggestions from federal executives and program managers, it is entirely understandable that the commission used private sector staffing standards. The yardstick is obviously suspect. Government operations are not business operations. To the extent that public management cannot or will not provide an alternative basis for assessing its own requirements, it is understandable that an ill-fitting measure was applied. Indeed, until public managers can establish a connection between productivity and personnel operations, invidious comparisons between public and private sectors will continue. The result will be unfortunate because the federal work force will suffer from the comparison.[16]

One problem plaguing discussions about improving the productivity of the public sector, however, is that at least three definitions of productivity compete for center stage. I believe that the three definitions derive from a complex relationship between government, politics, and management in which a three-sided relationship—not the classic, bipolar politics–administration continuum—produces three perspectives from which public productivity must be viewed.[17] The most visible perspective, and the one most prominent, is the view that applies efficiency criteria to bureaucratic operations. The efficiency view defines productivity according to the ratio of organizational products to resource outlays. Its contribution to discussions about productivity stems from its "volume up–cost down" concern for working faster and smarter to maximize organizational output for a given input or to minimize the resources required to reach fixed outputs.

Whether efficiency-based productivity programs work as intended remains to be seen. Some evidence suggests that narrowly conceived private sector programs are notably unproductive.[18] In the public sector, however, two arguments fuel the suspicion of efficiency-based definitions of productivity. One is the problem-solving view of public policy whose dominant concern is the effectiveness of government rather than its operational efficiency. The effectiveness view of productivity can be savage in its disregard for efficient administrative operations. What counts as productive behavior in this view is government's ability to solve practical public problems. Thus the effectiveness approach counts as productive activity that which neutralizes threats to public security; feeds the hungry; shelters and clothes citizens; treats the mentally and physically disabled; educates the work force; and encourages the development of viable commercial, transportation, and communications systems. This view of productivity is not the enemy

16. Alan K. Campbell, "The Institution and Its Problems," *Public Administration Review,* vol. 42 (July–August 1982), pp. 307–08.

17. Eugene B. McGregor, Jr., "The Public Service Problem," in *The Annals of the American Academy of Political and Social Science,* vol. 466 (March 1983), pp. 61–76.

18. Judson, "The Awkward Truth about Productivity," pp. 93–97.

of efficient agency practice. It is indifferent about whether government should supply public goods or services directly or remove itself from "private sector" activity that could produce the same results. What matters is the results!

The effectiveness critique of efficiency is joined by a third view of public productivity, the governance view. The foundation of the governance view stems from the processes through which productivity is achieved and the explicit recognition that large scale public action invariably involves a competitive and partisan exercise of power. Thus real world action requires policymakers to resolve questions of who wins and loses in the allocation of public goals and scarce resources.

The governance product eludes easy definition. It is both a final product and an intermediate product. It is a final product in the sense that democratic government and corollary freedoms are final justifications for governmental existence. Democratic self-government is also an instrumental product to the extent that an "intelligence of democracy" facilitates the discovery and pursuit of public productivity.[19] Thus the governance view discounts proposals for productivity improvement that do not include democratic policy processes in their list of aims. Indeed, the great irony in the governance perspective is that action taken in the name of efficiency and effectiveness can undermine the institutions on which democracy depends.[20] Clearly, the goals of operations efficiency, problem-solving effectiveness, and democratic governance are interconnected.

The structure of work force management

What is interesting about public service is that complex goal determinations are, in fact, made. Strategic planning—often of a very high order—does go on at all levels of government. Most of the strategic planning activity occurs at the bureau and agency level, however, and not at a governmentwide management level. Yet, personnel requirements stem from strategic definitions of productivity. Indeed, the whole problem of determining the requirements side of the work force management problem decomposes into three sets of problems. Each problem set represents the strategic, tactical, and operational choices confronting managerial decisionmakers.

The first and most significant set of choices involves policy decisions about organizational purposes and instruments. This is

19. Charles Lindbloom, *Intelligence of Democracy* (Free Press, 1965).
20. Jeffrey L. Pressman, *Federal Programs and City Politics: The Dynamics of the Aid Process in Oakland* (University of California Press, 1975).

the level of strategic decisionmaking. In private enterprise, for example, decisions to create new product lines, increase market shares for a product, cut production costs through automation, and advance the state of a particular technology affect work force requirements.[21] The decisions are strategic because they establish the size and skill mix of the labor pool needed to achieve primary organizational goals and objectives.

Obviously, government is disciplined by the same logic. For example, when governments fight wars, conduct research and development programs, stimulate economic development, or care for the indigent, personnel requirements result. When government decides that a competitive push must advance the state of the art in aerospace, sophisticated scientific and technical skills are required. When stimulating economic growth in depressed areas is the goal, entrepreneurial, financial, and industrial development skills are prized. If public policy moves capital into the construction of homes and offices, and into urban rehabilitation, then banking, insurance, and real estate skills are needed for successful execution of programs. If policy expands cash entitlement programs, then skills associated with computerized disbursement systems are required. If the aim is to expand the regulation of enterprise, then legal training and technically trained inspectors are needed to work on regulatory problems such as pollution control, environmental impact analysis, plant safety, and consumer product safety.

Mission requirements do not, by themselves, directly determine personnel operations in either public or private enterprise. For one thing, managerial decisionmakers still confront the strategic, "make or buy" decision of whether to implement programs and produce products in house or whether to contract out for the production mandated by the mission. Clearly, a decision to make products and services means that the enterprise must acquire production knowledge and skill. A decision to buy services and products means that the enterprise must either manage a procurement process or oversee projects and production processes operated by others.

The link between strategic decisionmaking (policymaking) and personnel operations is still not complete, however. A series of tactical decisions confront the manager. These decisions include the design and operation of an employment system within which work can be accomplished; the allocation and obligation of funds sufficient to cover human resource requirements; and the application of technology to the production process.

21. Tichy and others, "Strategic Human Resource Management," pp. 47–61.

Technology deserves further comment because it is used in both a strategic and a tactical sense in human resource management.[22] Technology acquires strategic significance when it defines the mission or goal of an agency or corporation. For example, when the mission of an organization is either to advance the state of knowledge or to develop prototypes and new products such as satellites, social service delivery models, or new construction methods, then the strategic policies of a firm or agency are at least partly defined by technology. Obviously, strategic choices of technology affect work force requirements.

The tactical issue by contrast involves organizational and managerial arrangements through which human resources are deployed. For example, if the goal is to advance the state of a given technology, then the resulting requirement is to organize people into teams attached to small-batch, nonroutine projects. By contrast, if the strategic aim is merely to produce as efficiently as possible those products and services for which the production requirements and markets are already known, then an organization's personnel can be deployed differently. Often, a labor force possessing routinized skills geared to the repetitive operations of large-batch, mass-produced production processes will be required.[23]

Furthermore, production (operations) technologies can vary. Managers can make tactical choices between labor-intensive, nonmechanized technology and capital-intensive, mechanized technology. For example, in insurance companies, banks, and government entitlement programs (for example, social security, unemployment insurance, aid to families with dependent children), the management of accounts and the disbursement of funds can be done either by clerks working through cases by hand or by computers disbursing funds according to programmed rules and electronically managed financial transfers.

Clearly, personnel requirements are directly affected by tactical decisions about production technology. In the labor-intensive option, case workers and an army of clerks will be needed. In the capital-intensive application of computer technology, computer technicians, systems analysts, and auditors working with the electronic storage and retrieval of data files will be required. Once

22. Charles Perrow, *Complex Organizations: A Critical Essay* (Scott, Foresman and Company, 1973).

23. Joan Woodward, *Industrial Organization: Theory and Practice* (Oxford University Press, 1965); and Paul Lawrence and Jay Lorsch, *Organizations and Environment* (Harvard University Press, 1967).

again, strategic and tactical problems must be resolved before beginning to address the issues of managing personnel operations.

Thus far, two conclusions are indicated. First, once strategic, tactical, and operational decisions are made, the vast majority of all personnel decisions are also made. Regrettably, many such decisions are made without consulting personnel specialists.

Second, the link between public productivity and personnel is complex and cannot be analyzed by simple, efficiency measures. Indeed, not only is it difficult to analyze the link between public products and public employees, the link has a counterintuitive side. Increasing only nominal efficiency of personnel operations in the short term can undermine government productivity in the long term. For example, reform of the federal retirement system carries a prospective three-year savings potential of more than $58 billion. Clearly, lowering the pension benefit level, extending the retirement age, and changing inflation indexing are tempting targets for productivity improvement. What is not clear is the effect of pension reform on personnel operations. Across-the-board pension reductions without adjustments in the total compensation package may make career government service less attractive at precisely the time that the federal government requires a more sophisticated work force. Extending the period over which employees are locked in a pension system also increases the training and development costs needed to maintain and update the skills of an aging work force. Thus many of the most tempting proposals to improve productivity are problematic and require careful study.

The federal approach

Documenting the absence of federal work force management is more difficult than demonstrating what might now be done. Urging the establishment of a new agency—such as a Federal Management Agency—in the Executive Office of the President only begs the question: What would such an agency contribute to the management of the federal system?

The following list is an attempt to answer the question. The list includes functions not now performed by central management agencies.

—Designing a management information system for federal personnel;

—Designing total compensation systems for the federal work force based on salary survey data;

—Developing productivity-based performance appraisal guidelines that can be adapted to the needs of particular agencies;

—Overseeing staffing standards research, which is the key to the establishment of work force requirements;

—Designing and managing work force development programs designed to facilitate the conversion of federal personnel into an effective postindustrial work force;

—Overseeing governmentwide forecasting and planning; and

—Offering technical assistance to strengthen work force management in various departments and agencies.

The list is intended to be tendentious; it defines managerial activity rather than the current operational concerns of the OPM and the OMB.

To summarize, it seems clear that public managers must assess personnel operations based on productivity requirements. Such analysis would compare strategic personnel requirements with the availability of on-board personnel and formulate strategies by which the two sides of the personnel equation can be balanced. Practitioners must break new ground. As noted earlier, literature that describes in practical terms how to accomplish the tasks of balancing requirements and supplies in the work force is scant, presenting a state-of-the-art challenge to scholars and practitioners alike.

Finally, a real knowledge gap occurs on the requirements side of the equation, particularly in the determination of staffing standards. Little progress can be made in the art of work force management without linking strategic planning and the operational demand for human resources.

Continuous reform

A sustained drive to improve government personnel operations is justified for many reasons. Without a managerially based system of personnel administration, the federal work force remains vulnerable to any faction that alleges overpayment, overstaffing, and a lack of excellence. Self-protection is one reason that a prudent work force will want to submit to a careful, productivity-based scrutiny of its operations. One of two results will occur. Either analysts will discover opportunities for cost savings, or they will not. If they do, opportunities will arise to exchange less effective practices for more effective practices without compromising the productivity goals of government. If analysts see no opportunity for cost savings, then federal executives can defend personnel practices based on proven rather than unproven government operating requirements.

Another advantage of rigorous, managerial oversight of the federal work force is that public policymakers are entitled to know how many federal workers are needed to run government programs under alternative strategies. The idea that any administration—Republican or Democratic—will finance a large bureaucratic mystery whose practices and products remain obscure to those who pay for the enterprise is unrealistic. The current evidence suggests that fiscally constrained policymakers are willing to boil the bureaucratic beast down until convinced of the need to finance personnel, programs, and offices. In such an environment, federal executives and managers will find it in their interest to insure that a continuous managerial review of personnel practice occurs. Periodic external reviews of governmental practice could convince an unappreciative public that putative management excellence is legitimate. External review can do no damage and is potentially useful in documenting improvements.

Finally, at least speculatively, the productivity of the federal work force is the hidden key to effective management of the rest of the federal budget. Enormous damage and waste occur when large, expensive national programs are mismanaged. It takes only a little imagination, for example, to envision a scenario in which the implementation of the Grace Commission's reforms could lead to a flight of top talent from federal service, a long-term rise in the costs of those programs that survive federal budget cuts, and an increase in the contracting out of federal government sovereignty and ability to manage public policy. In other words, an insensitive adoption of the Grace personnel recommendations can result in less productivity rather than more productivity even as the proposals advertise short-term, nominal savings.

The following points are made for the sake of discussion. I believe that implementing them would lead to short-term improvement in the management of federal personnel.

Restructure the federal personnel information system. The system should include productivity criteria. The revised information structure should distinguish position, person, and product-based personnel classifications. Reorganize the current structure of series and groups that now serves only operational personnel interests, keeping in mind the productive contribution of federal personnel.

Begin to develop staffing standards. Initiate staffing standards research that would support productivity analyses and work force planning.

Consider revising the current position-based system of white-collar employment. Assess the desirability of flexible classification and compensation systems. Each system would be supported by appropriate performance management systems that recognize multiple compensation criteria.

Assess the development of staffing plans. Such plans should be an integral part of policy development, the budget process, and personnel operations management. Staffing plans would be required to document the personnel needs of various agencies. Base the plans on actions needed to balance work force requirements and on-board availability.

Ironically, the Grace Commission has seriously underestimated the stakes of the personnel management exercise. Whether $91 billion (the high estimate) in direct personnel costs can be saved over the next three years obscures the real issue. The real question is whether the federal government will retain a work force adequate for the size and sophistication of the programs, agencies, and instruments that now serve national public policy. If improving national productivity is the primary concern, then the stakes of the Grace Commission challenge to public personnel administration involve more than the savings estimate.

General Discussion

IRVING H. DEARNLEY, vice-president of Citibank, North America, and a member of the Grace Commission's task force on personnel management, began the discussion by outlining the basic approach that was followed by the task force. He said that it was essentially the same approach that he would follow in doing a comprehensive study of the Citibank system. He observed that the federal government lacks the marketplace discipline of competition in determining its pay and benefits structure; therefore, private sector practices can serve as a surrogate.

Dearnley observed that a retirement plan, whether public or private sector, should be intended to provide an orderly means of retirement for older employees. The plan should provide a measure of financial security that is on the average competitive with that provided by major competitors for employment. It should take into consideration both social security and some portion of personal savings so that the system approximates the income needed to maintain the preretirement standard of living for career employees without being excessive. In addition, the retirement system should consider an employee's contribution to the organization in terms of years of service and the employee's salary at the point of retirement. Furthermore, the system should be favorably regarded by employees and retirees. Dearnley said that in the absence of a stated civil service retirement objective, the commission recommends use of these guidelines.

Dearnley said that estimates of cost under a retirement plan involve establishing economic and actuarial assumptions reaching many years into the future and detailed information concerning the demographics of employees and annuitants. He conceded that there was not enough time in the three months at the task force's disposal to make precise estimates of cost savings from its recommendations and said that the task force has proposed that such estimates be undertaken by the Office of the Actuary (in the Office of Personnel Management).

60

Dwight Ink, former executive director of the President's (Carter's) Personnel Management Project, began the discussion by saying that he had mixed impressions of the Grace Commission report. He said that the report succeeds in bringing a high level of attention to some problems of government, particularly on the part of the president, that is badly needed. But the Grace Commission misfired on some of the basic causes of these problems. Although the Grace Commission is correct on issues like management disincentives in the system, it gave inadequate recognition to the negative impact of poor and sometimes untrained leadership in the federal government. Citing the Synthetic Fuels Corporation as an example, Ink pointed to the lack of management experience at top management levels and the heavy load on administrative personnel responding to oversight questions from Congress, the General Accounting Office, and Inspector Generals.

Ink observed that 8,000 pages of personnel regulations, 2,000 pages of federal procurement regulations, interest group pressure, and oversight investigations confront federal managers. Private sector firms do not have to contend with such pressures. He felt that the Grace Commission's recommendation to establish an Office of Federal Management would only worsen the problem. By greatly enlarging the Office of Management and Budget (OMB), the commission would leave management functions with budget functions under the mistaken view that budget improvement initiatives help management. But in the OMB, budget considerations increasingly overwhelm management concerns. Placing the OPM, the General Services Administration (GSA), and the OMB two levels down in an Office of Federal Management produces an unacceptable amount of layering in a critical area. The head of the OPM now has limited access to the president; the Grace Commission's recommendation would virtually eliminate that access. Even a greatly streamlined OPM and GSA would, in Ink's judgment, place far too many people in the Executive Office of the President and produce an unmanageable amount of detail for the Executive Office of the President.

Ink closed by saying that there are some important things to salvage from the survey on cost control such as the general direction of work force planning and some changes in the retirement system that are inevitable.

Wesley Liebtag, director of personnel programs at IBM, said that he thought the conferees would do well to concentrate on things that should be done and stay away from the particular politics and problems of the Grace Commission. He doubted that there was anyone in the room who would not agree that a change in the management characteristics of the federal government is needed. To make such changes, leadership, down to the middle management levels, is essential. Major change can only come with the intelligent, honest, moral commitment of the managers in the federal government. He stated that he saw little of such commitment.

A key to building ownership of the problem of federal management and leadership, Liebtag said, is a general focus on education and training of the people involved. Citing the difficulty of getting top federal executives to executive seminars, he argued that the situation must be changed and leadership education institutionalized.

David Stanley, a former senior fellow at Brookings, asked McGregor how the federal government might institutionalize the overall approach to providing better information and a better philosophy to solve its personnel problems.

Eugene McGregor responded that there are three basic choices to pursue: strengthen the OPM by assigning a group within the OPM to work on the problem; put a greater managerial emphasis into the OMB; or create a new arena for thinking about management.

McGregor suggested that the government try to improve its information. A good place to start is by improving the occupational classification system to make it more useful to managers. Because of the increasing professionalization of the work force, agencies are having to use classification as a way to solve pay problems, which is one of the problems of overgrading. McGregor also mentioned learning how to use the data available for work force planning purposes.

Ink commented on Stanley's institutionalization question with two suggestions. First, the federal government must find a better way of appointing political executives, particularly choosing people who know how to operate large organizations. Such people should be skilled at selecting people to fill positions of responsibility, and they should appreciate the importance of employee and executive development. Second, employee development must be much broader than formal training; development includes education on the job. Ink observed that this issue was largely ignored by both the Civil Service Reform Act and the Grace Commission.

Bradley Patterson, a senior staff member at Brookings, asked McGregor how he would handle the problem of ambiguous goals in government programs.

McGregor responded that there is a massive contradiction in the Grace Commission report that implies that one gets more product by shrinking the inputs relative to what people are normally doing. The problem is that one also changes the skill mix of the work force in order to get that same product. Because it takes a very sophisticated work force to run a contracting system, it is hard to sustain the government's in-house capacity for management when large amounts of the work have been contracted to entities outside the government. The problem in the Grace Commission's logic is that if one tries to improve public productivity suddenly by cutting personnel costs and rapidly shrinking government employment, it becomes difficult to sustain the skill mix supportive of both specialized technical competence and effective contract management. The irony is that the commission understated the payout; the benefits of successful work force management might be much larger over time than the $91 billion the Grace Commission seeks to save. In other words, the payoff period of good personnel management may be forever, and the cost of poor choices astronomical.

O. Glen Stahl remarked that no one had mentioned that installing a number of changes, such as better information, better oversight, and more intensive executive training, will cost money. And, cost is one reason that these ideas were not instituted many years ago when they should have been. He said that even though they do not cost a great deal of money in the long run, out-of-pocket expenditures capture the attention and negative reactions of politicians and the people they represent. As a result, reaching compromises as to what the government should do will not be easy.

A. Lee Fritschler observed that improving techniques of personnel management is clearly an area where the private sector can contribute enormously to government. However, government may not be able to involve itself in what corporations have traditionally thought of as strategic management and strategic planning. He wondered whether the Grace Commission might have made more of a contribution if it had gone to some intermediate level. For example, could the commission have recommended how to cut away some of the underbrush that impedes the public manager?

Liebtag answered that he thought it was a matter of definition. In his understanding of McGregor's argument, McGregor was talking about balancing off resource needs.

McGregor added that the logic of work force planning requires that one work from a strategic to a tactical to an operational calculation about the development of human resources to meet strategic goals. The difficult part is to determine the staffing standard. The purpose of work force management is cause a conversation about which people are needed to run certain kinds of programs. A starting place for this activity is determining what kind of work force one has and what the work force is really doing. Computers really don't enter the picture until one has the capacity to ask the right questions.

Fritschler observed that one of the differences between the public and private sectors is the need to maintain two sets of books: things to do that make sense from a management standpoint, and things that must be done from a political standpoint. Implementation of the first set of things is often impossible.

Ink responded that he thought that points up the importance of the penalty paid for a lack of continuity in the federal government and the lack of competent leadership at the political level.

Comarow spoke of his experiences with the Ash Council in 1969 and 1970, which came to the conclusion that not only does the government not have an overall personnel management system, it doesn't even have an overall management system. And, he said, the Ash Council found deficiencies in information systems and executive training and development, as had several previous task forces and commissions. The important question is, why has this happened?

He said the answer is leadership, especially the quality of the top managers of an agency. He wondered why the Grace Commission failed to address the question of what one does in a political democracy, where the managers at the first three or four levels often—not always, but often—come unprepared and un-qualified to do their jobs and stay for an average of about two years.

Liebtag responded that he didn't see that issue as part of the Grace Commission's charge. He related the issue of leadership to education, underscoring the importance of top management support for executive education.

Patrick Korten remarked that the issue was not one of leadership but of cost control. He said that the question to answer is, does a system in which these leaders operate inhibit or promote their ability to lead? The Grace Commission was offering a means of improving the system so that leadership could have a better chance to succeed.

Ink responded that the issue isn't political leadership—that's essential in a democracy. He said there are many good managers in the Republican Party and the Democratic Party, and that any administration can find the loyalty a president must have and still fill his political population with people who understand how to operate large organizations.

Ronald Moe added that the issue is that the political appointment process has gone too far down in many agencies. Most decisions at most agencies over time are really not partisan decisions. Top political leaders should realize that most professionals are there to serve the president, and those employees can do so more often and better than many of the political appointees. He said that the Grace Commission failed to discuss a real and legitimate problem in this regard. What positions should be left to political appointees, and what positions should properly be left to career civil servants?

Edward C. Gallas, vice-president, Organization Resources Counsellors, observed that given the political constraints on federal personnel management policy, the Grace Commission aimed at too broad a level of policy change. He said that managers should be given more authority to manage their staff. Personnel functions need to be decentralized.

Charles Levine said that if one follows some of McGregor's logic and accepts Gallas's prescription that personnel management should be decentralized, then the personnel offices in federal agencies will have to change. He wondered what the new offices might look like.

McGregor responded that on one hand the design of the executive branch is largely premised on strong bureaus and agencies. On the other hand, there is a great suspicion of strong central controls except for operational controls on personnel practice lodged in the OPM and average grade and employment controls given to the Office of Management and Budget. To begin to improve federal personnel management in a way that bridges the OPM and the OMB, start with good information. To do that, a small group of people should begin to answer some of the questions raised by the survey on cost control. Then begin the analysis by attaching some requirement-side questions concerning programs and products to this information base. Next ask some questions about staffing standards—about how discrepancies between public and private sector staffing arise. What is likely to occur is a realization that the present position management system can be replaced with a system that rewards employees for productivity rather than for the positions they hold. Compensation systems ought to be modified with less restrictive guidelines that would allow merit pay to be driven by professional and production standards as opposed to position, job-based factors, and benchmarks used in the present system.

McGregor said that the work force needs to be decomposed into categories that, for example, would allow separate schedules for scientists and engineers. As a result, the government could escape the practice of using across-the-board raises, which creates large aggregate numbers but not necessarily appropriate pay. McGregor concluded that if this sort of office and information were generated, the classic American strategy of relying on the bureaus and agencies level for policymaking and management would be reinforced.

Ink added that these numbers can be useful. When used by the General Accounting Office, Inspector Generals, and the congressional committees, they become guidelines that can often be used to control agency decisionmaking.

James Mitchell, a former member of the Civil Service Commission, asked McGregor to comment on the lack of attention devoted to the operating side of personnel management in the Grace Commission report and cited promotion systems as an example. He asked if McGregor thought that the federal service was doing reasonably well.

McGregor said that often having looked at a number of agencies and their field centers, he was frankly impressed. The real strength of the system is in operational procedures set in place many years ago. As a result, the system can provide information useful to a work force management effort.

Ink added that how the situation is perceived is important. The issue is whether one is looking at where we are now and how far we have come or if one is looking at where we need to go. On the one hand, he would tend to agree with the Grace Commission that there is a long way to go. On the other hand, given the complexity of the federal government, it's not surprising that these kinds of changes take time before the personnel management system attains anything like the objectives that are hoped for.

John D. Harris, assistant to the national president, American Federation of Government Employees, observed that throughout most of the discussion participants had been operating under the assumption that the way to get a better management system is to use more central controls or to establish a central institution. What would happen if instead of 6,000 pages of regulations, an Office of Personnel Management or Office of Federal Management, and the General Services Administration, personnel management is transferred to the federal managers who would manage in accordance with their judgment and education?

Ink responded that he didn't think that the situation is an either/or one. He referred to the National Academy of Public Administration's report on revitalizing federal management and said the report concluded that the system is much too complex. More responsibility should be delegated to the agencies and within the agencies. He also said that the strategic role of the central agencies, the Office of Personnel Management, and the academy's version of an Office of Federal Management must be strengthened. There must be a better way through which presidential leadership can be exercised, in order to decentralize effectively.

Harris asked how Ink would feel about simply decentralizing the authority to establish individual agency-level compensation systems; that is, an authority at the agency level to design and establish personnel systems, with respect to compensation.

Ink responded that he would retain a governmentwide system but within that system, he would create broader ranges so that the agencies had greater flexibility. He said in this instance he would move more in the direction of what most corporations do.

Liebtag said that some things are not amenable to perfection. He cited three examples. One, the distribution of people throughout a grade level is never satisfactory. A good rule is, less is better. Use the lowest average grade level needed to get the job done and to satisfy the people involved. Two, neither industry nor government will ever be happy with the appraisal skew. Everybody will always try to cheat. So changing the appraisal system to get a better skew is a waste of time. Finally, no one will ever be satisfied with the job descriptions used, and no one will ever be satisfied with the number of level grades or categories. There are no perfect numbers in personnel management.

McGregor responded that the central problem is that the questions that management needs to answer cannot be answered when the emphasis in personnel management is only on control. Information that aids decisionmaking and solves problems must be assembled.

Dearnley commented that from a corporate standpoint the

personnel system should be as decentralized as possible, insuring that personnel people are sensitive to the needs of that particular business. However, some policy issues demand more corporate-wide integration; in many corporations there is a corporate personnel group. But, he added, the group focuses mainly on overall policies that are within a framework suitable for individual businesses. In general, the business sector favors decentralization, not centralization.

The Grace Commission and Civil Service Reform: Seeking a Common Understanding

 PERSONNEL management in the federal government is a favorite subject for reform. From commission to task force to improvement council, every administration starts afresh to diagnose the most serious problems plaguing the civil service and to propose solutions, or at least directions for change. Two of the most far-reaching recent efforts are President Jimmy Carter's civil service reforms of 1978 and President Ronald Reagan's Private Sector Survey on Cost Control, better known as the Grace Commission.[1]

The Carter initiatives produced extensive changes in the federal civil service. In 1979 the Office of Personnel Management was established, along with the Merit Systems Protection Board and the Federal Labor Relations Authority. The Senior Executive Service came into being, along with a new research and demonstration authority pertaining to personnel management and new approaches to hiring, appraising, rewarding, and firing employees. The Grace Commission proposes equally dramatic steps that largely remain at the discussion stage. Eight of the commission's eighteen clusters of personnel management recommendations deal with employee benefits. Taken together, the recommendations on benefits are the most extensive of the Grace Commission's proposals in anticipated dollar savings to the government, although the accuracy of the savings estimated is questionable.[2]

Other Grace Commission recommendations concern the Senior Executive Service (SES), management practice more generally, and the systematic study of personnel management initiatives.

---

1. Pub.L. 95–454 (October 13, 1978) and Presidential Reorganization Plan Number 2 of 1978; President's Private Sector Survey on Cost Control, J. Peter Grace, chairman, *War on Waste* (Macmillan, 1984) (Hereafter Grace, *War on Waste*.). For greater detail on the Grace Commission's proposals, see President's Private Sector Survey on Cost Control, *Report on Personnel Management* and *Report on Federal Management Systems, Working Appendix* (Hereafter *Report on Federal Management Systems*) (Washington, D.C.: PPSSCC, 1983).

2. *Report of the Task Force on Personnel Management of the President's Private Sector Survey on Cost Control,* Hearing before the Subcommittee on Investigations of the House Committee on Post Office and Civil Service, 98 Cong. 1 sess. (Government Printing Office, 1983); and U.S. Congressional Budget Office and U.S. General Accounting Office (GAO), *Analysis of the Grace Commission's Major Proposals for Cost Control* (GPO, 1984).

Although not expected to produce large direct dollar savings, these other recommendations are acknowledged in the Grace Commission report to have substantial indirect effects on government efficiency. Strong leadership and improved knowledge are also important to government performance more generally.[3]

This essay assesses the recommendations of the Grace Commission in light of recent experience with the Civil Service Reform Act of 1978 (CSRA) and related reorganizations. The central question is, what lessons do experiences under the 1978 reforms offer as the desirability and feasibility of the commission's proposals are considered? The first section of this essay examines three goals common to both the Grace Commission and the CSRA: attracting and retaining the best executive talent; giving federal managers the necessary tools to manage well; and strengthening the place of research, demonstrations, and program evaluation in the federal government. The second section steps back from the specific goals and proposals to consider a central assumption of the commission's endeavor—that private sector strategies and experience can and should be adopted by the public sector.

Three goals of reform

The CSRA and the Grace Commission's proposals share three important concerns. Both reforms identify problems with the federal government's ability to attract and retain executives,, encourage good management practice more generally, and conduct needed studies of personnel management innovations. These three concerns appear over and over again in assessments of federal government practice by the General Accounting Office, the National Academy of Public Administration, and earlier commissions. As problems, they are worth grappling with, since the quality of management and research is significant to government performance overall.

Despite their importance, solutions to these problems are neither obvious nor simple to effect. Changes implemented under the CSRA were expected to help, but the CSRA's successes have been modest. The Grace Commission offers additional suggestions, some of which may undo progress already achieved.

Attracting and Retaining Executive Talent

The Grace Commission's *Report on Personnel Management* identifies severe problems at the upper end of the federal personnel

---

3. PPSSCC, *Report on Personnel Management,* pp. 112, 193.

system: pay compression, inadequate salaries, low morale, premature retirement, and dissatisfaction with the executive bonus system. To address these problems, members of the commission propose that the SES should shrink in size and that top executive salaries should be raised. Each recommendation merits discussion, along with another Grace Commission proposal to abolish any carry over of annual leave from one year to the next.

The Grace Commission report recommends that the Office of Personnel Management (OPM) study the positions included in the SES, with the expectation that such a study will propose a smaller executive corps.[4] Grace's explicit justification for concern about excessive size is that SES members without executive-level responsibilities might be receiving bonuses, thereby diverting money from others whose work merits bonus recognition.[5] This concern is overdrawn, however, since studies have consistently shown that lower-level members of the SES are much less likely than their senior colleagues to receive bonuses.[6]

The commission's unstated reasons for shrinking the SES may include a simple desire to cut costs—fewer people at high salaries cost less—or a belief that raising top executive salaries would be difficult to accomplish politically without simultaneously reducing the number of executives overall. In principle, the size of the SES and the levels of executive pay are separable; there are several salary levels now for executives, and there could be a much greater spread between the top and the bottom. Admittedly, in the past there has rarely been a large spread in executive pay, and pay caps have shrunk the spread even more. However, the success of the Reagan administration in raising top executives' pay by nearly 40 percent demonstrates that past practice need not serve as a guide for future action.

Neither the explicit justification nor the implicit justification of the Grace Commission for shrinking the size of the SES is particularly persuasive. One likely consequence of shrinkage, not considered by the Grace Commission, is controversial and runs counter to a central goal of the CSRA: a smaller SES would reduce the amount of assignment flexibility that the CSRA gives to agency heads. A bit of civil service reform history is relevant.

Prior to the CSRA, federal personnel rules made it difficult for political appointees to move career executives from one job to

4. Ibid., pp. 112–120.
5. Ibid., p. 117.
6. GAO, "Testimony of the Comptroller General on the Impact of the Senior Executive Service" (GAO/GGD-84-32, December 30, 1983), p. 4.

another. Reassignments were restricted to positions of the same grade and rank. Since there were few positions at the GS–17 and GS–18 levels, especially outside of the Washington, D.C., area, careerists at these high levels were difficult to reassign and almost impossible to move geographically.[7] The CSRA changed this. Under today's rank-in-person system in the SES, there is no longer any requirement to distinguish among executive positions in terms of grade or rank. Any career (permanent) executive can be assigned to virtually any SES position. Today, executives can be moved easily to positions of greater or lesser responsibility, or moved geographically, without long delays, extensive justifications, or appeals.[8] A majority of positions in the SES are classified as general, which means they can be filled by either a career or noncareer (political appointee) executive. That classification opens many positions to noncareer appointees that were formerly restricted to members of the career service. With more than 8,000 SES positions authorized by the OPM, reassignment flexibility is considerable.

A large pool of jobs included in the SES means that there are out-of-the-way places where career executives can be assigned and that many key staff and line positions are available for noncareer appointees. In areas of high priority, several layers of positions can be filled by political appointees, enhancing the ability of agency heads to control programs, a goal of the CSRA.

In addition, since the number of noncareer appointees is statutorily limited to 10 percent of the authorized SES positions governmentwide, the more positions authorized for the SES, the larger the permissible number of noncareer executive appointments. The number of noncareer appointees under the Reagan administration has remained below the statutory limit but has exceeded 10 percent of the on-board executive population (because of vacant executive positions). In some agencies, the ratio of noncareer executives to career executives has increased markedly

7. As of March 31, 1978, the proportion of GS–17 employees assigned to positions outside of the Washington, D.C., area was 18 percent, and one in ten employees at the GS–18 level worked outside the D.C. area. See U.S. Civil Service Commission, *Pay Structure of the Federal Civil Service* (GPO, 1978), p. 36.

8. Executives can appeal their reassignments on the grounds that they were reassigned based upon a prohibited personnel practice. See Toni Marzotto, Carolyn Ban, and Edie Goldenberg, "Controlling the U.S. Federal Bureaucracy: Will the Senior Executive Service Make a Difference?" in G.E. Caiden and H. Siedentopf, eds., *Strategies for Administrative Reform* (Lexington, 1982).

under this administration, but it has done so within the boundaries set by the CSRA.[9]

Increasing assignment flexibility was one of the central goals of establishing the SES and has been one of its clearest accomplishments. Today, a greater number of political appointees can occupy a wider array of positions than before the SES, and executive vacancies can be filled faster. Perhaps the CSRA goes too far, including positions in the SES that should be kept beyond direct political control. Perhaps some positions require such high levels of technical expertise that they do not belong in an SES system that assumes that any executive is competent to hold any job.

Shrinking the size of the SES would reduce managerial flexibility and limit political control to a smaller number of people and positions. This likely result is not mentioned in the Grace Commission report. It is a result at odds with the overall philosophy of the commission—to fashion the federal government more in the likeness of a hierarchical, private sector enterprise. Limits on political control of federal departments and agencies are rarely popular with those currently in office. Perhaps that explains why the recommendation to shrink the SES has received such a quiet reception from this otherwise cost-conscious administration.

Raising executive pay is another priority of the Grace Commission. The commission proposes raising the pay of top executives by 20 to 30 percent and separating executive from congressional pay setting.[10] The idea of separate pay setting, which has also been supported by the General Accounting Office (GAO),[11] was discussed and rejected at the time of the civil service reforms. The designers of the CSRA believed that Congress and congressional staff would resist setting executive salaries higher than their own. Therefore, the reform act's designers assumed that decoupling executive and congressional salary adjustments would do little to encourage higher executive salaries. On one hand, the linkage of executive and congressional pay protects federal executives who eventually do receive pay increases once congressional salaries increase. On the other hand, the linkage protects congres-

9. Edie N. Goldenberg, "The Permanent Government in an Era of Retrenchment and Redirection," in Lester M. Salamon and Michael S. Lund, eds., *The Reagan Presidency and the Governing of America* (Urban Institute Press, 1984).

10. PPSSCC, *Report on Personnel Management,* pp. 113–22.

11. GAO, "Annual Adjustments—The Key to Federal Executive Pay" (GAO/FPCD-79-31, May 17, 1979).

sional salaries, which can be raised by arguing the need for higher executive pay. That rationale may be hard for Congress to give up.[12]

Separating executive and legislative pay setting is an idea worth reconsidering, even though the political prospects for passing successful legislation are discouraging. Salary separation offers the only realistic way to make executive salary adjustments more regular. Annual adjustments would smooth the current lumpiness of retirement decisions based on high-three calculations, a desirable result. Moreover, fears of resistance to executive pay rates higher than congressional salaries are probably exaggerated. Similar fears were widespread at the time the CSRA was first passed—that military officers would be unwilling to grant bonuses to their civilian subordinates if, with bonuses, the civilians would earn more than their military supervisors. Experience under the CSRA has shown that such fears are groundless.

There is broad agreement that top executive salaries are too low.[13] They are not commensurate with executive responsibilities, and they fall far short of the salaries for comparable positions in the private sector. One of the most underreported achievements of the Reagan administration has been its success in raising top executive salaries by over one-third. This achievement helped stem the exodus of top executives, who were retiring from public service at an alarming rate.[14] However, because of the high-three retirement system, which calculates benefits based on the highest three years of salary, Reagan might only have delayed the exodus until three years following the large salary increases (unless subsequent increases are also forthcoming). If the Grace Commission's proposals to alter retirement benefit calculations to a high five were implemented, executives might stay longer in the public service between pay raises.[15]

Raising executive pay is also a concern of the CSRA, which

12. My thanks to James Cowan for clarifying this point.

13. GAO, "Federal Executive Pay Compression Worsens: Report to the Congress" (GAO/FPCD-800-72, July 31, 1980); Statement of Dr. Donald J. Devine, Director of the Office of Personnel Management, *Government Brain Drain,* Hearing before the Subcommittee on Civil Service, Post Office, and General Services of the Senate Committee on Governmental Affairs, 97 Cong. 1 sess. (GPO, 1981), pp. 153–72.

14. Goldenberg, "The Permanent Government in an Era of Retrenchment and Redirection."

15. The short-run impact of such a change in retirement calculation could be to accelerate departures from the government as employees retire quickly before the new rules go into effect. However, once the transition period is past, a high-five system should encourage employees to work longer.

established a separate pay system for senior executives and a system to award lump-sum bonuses up to 20 percent of basic salary. The Grace Commission report notes the poor morale in the executive ranks and the lack of credibility of the bonus system[16] but offers no specific suggestions for improving either one.

The executive bonus system has not measured up to anyone's expectations, perhaps because initial expectations were vague, unrealistic, and contradictory. The designers of the CSRA were never clear about the purpose of executive bonuses. People were allowed to develop incompatible expectations about how, and by what criteria, bonuses would be awarded, a situation destined to produce disappointment. Key members of Congress resisted the idea of using bonuses to circumvent congressionally imposed pay caps, so the bonus provisions were justified as a way to reward and promote outstanding performance. Nevertheless, the high statutory limit (50 percent) on the proportion of executives eligible in any year to receive bonuses created the impression that most executives would receive a bonus at least every few years. Furthermore, just after CSRA was signed into law, the OPM policy leaders suggested that as many as two-thirds of an agency's career executives could be eligible for bonuses in any one year. The 50 percent limit was based upon the total number of SES positions, which includes both vacancies and positions filled by noncareer appointees who are ineligible to receive bonuses. Not surprisingly, congressional staff balked at that interpretation. The OPM was forced to tone down its enthusiasm. Nevertheless, when the first agencies awarded bonuses to the maximum number of eligible executives, the awards precipitated an uproar on Capitol Hill that nearly killed the whole bonus program. The result was a severe limitation on the number and size of bonuses, cutting the 50 percent limit to 20 percent for the first few years.[17]

The extensive comments on bonuses in the 1984 hearings before the House Committee on Post Office and Civil Service[18] expose the confusion that exists over the purpose of executive bonuses. Are they meant to recognize excellence in past performance? If so, then why does the General Accounting Office resist the idea

16. PPSSCC, *Report on Personnel Management*, pp. 114–15.

17. See Marzotto and others, "Controlling the U.S. Federal Bureaucracy." Under legislation passed in late 1984, bonuses are no longer limited to a percentage of the executives in an agency. Instead, agencies have greater flexibility to award bonuses out of a bonus pool calculated as a percentage of SES payroll.

18. *Senior Executive Service*, Hearings before the Subcommittee on Civil Service of the House Committee on Post Office and Civil Service, 98 Cong. 1 sess. (GPO, 1984).

of awarding them to reemployed annuitants?[19] And, why is it shocking when big award winners leave the government soon after receiving their money? Initially, the GAO recommended that demonstrated performance be used as the sole basis for awarding bonuses; subsequently, the GAO has supported using other factors besides performance in making bonus decisions.[20]

Are bonuses meant to stimulate excellence in future performance? If so, why not award them and pay them over time only to those who continue to serve? In reality bonuses have been used to recruit employees for the federal service, to compensate for difficult or unpleasant assignments, to bring prestige to programs, to retain executives who might otherwise leave, to substitute for adequate pay distinctions between levels, and to accomplish a variety of other purposes as well. Such varied uses are common in the private sector, where the bonus idea originated. If SES bonuses are meant to be used as they are in business, then criticism of such uses is inappropriate.

Understanding the history of the bonus provision is instructive in two ways. First, some approaches to raising executive pay can backfire. Rather than making executive service more attractive, the bonus system created unfulfilled expectations and serious morale problems. If the Grace Commission's proposal moves forward to separate executive and legislative pay setting, it should do so without exaggerated promises of subsequent pay boosts for federal executives.

Second, disappointments with the bonus system are also important to an understanding of the significance of annual leave accumulation for members of the SES.[21] The CSRA introduced changes to allow members of the SES to accumulate annual leave indefinitely and to receive a cash payment for unused leave when exiting from public service. This was another of the sweeteners to induce executives to join the SES and to give up the security they formerly enjoyed regarding assignments. The controversy over bonuses, which led to a temporary scaling back of the bonus program, left many SES members feeling betrayed. Eliminating the other major inducement for joining the SES—leave accumulation and its cashing out at termination of service—may undermine morale even further and discourage experienced career

19. GAO, "Actions Needed to Enhance the Credibility of the Senior Executive Service Performance Award Programs" (GAO/FPCD-81-65, September 30, 1981).

20. GAO, "Actions Needed to Enhance the Credibility of the Senior Executive Service"; and GAO, "Testimony," p. 4.

21. PPSSCC, *Report on Personnel Management*, pp. 70, 71.

managers from seeking executive responsibility. Admittedly, the large size of some of the annual leave accumulations poses a potential problem, since paying tens of thousands of dollars to exiting executives may prove awkward politically. To lessen this problem, the OPM recommends periodic cashing out of annual leave accumulations. This seems an intelligent approach, balancing the need to attract and retain executive talent against political realities.

In sum, the Grace Commission joins with the CSRA in a harmonious call for higher executive salaries but links pay to a smaller SES without fully considering the likely consequences. Higher pay for top federal executives is certainly an important and worthy goal, but reformers should avoid raising expectations beyond what can be delivered. Finally, unless members of the SES are exempted from the Grace Commission's proposed reductions in employee benefits, such as reduced annual leave accumulation, the commission's recommendations as a whole have the potential to undermine executive morale still further, thereby exacerbating one of the most serious problems in federal personnel management today.

Improving Management Practice

Beyond proposals directed solely at the executive ranks, the Grace Commission also emphasizes good management practice throughout the federal government. A common message of the commission reports and the CSRA is that there is too little emphasis at the top levels of the government on management skills, that line managers have too little flexibility and authority to do their jobs, and that no systematic feedback system exists to provide managers with information on employees' opinions.

The Grace Commission task force on federal management systems states the obvious—that the rapid turnover of key executives in government makes continuity of management difficult to achieve, management improvements difficult to sustain, and attention to long-term thinking difficult to encourage. Since public problems often take years to address effectively, attempts to hold short-term managers accountable for organizational performance encourage managerial attention to immediate fixes rather than to investments in long-term solutions.

To strengthen management leadership in the federal government, the Grace Commission proposes a reorganization of central management agency functions into an Office of Federal Management (OFM). The OFM would include OMB's budgetary responsibilities and in addition would be responsible for policy development and direction in financial management, budgeting and planning, human resources, administration, and management improvement. The General Services Administration and the OPM would report to the OFM for policy direction in their respective areas.[22] Most personnel management operations would be delegated to the departments and agencies, leaving the OPM with certain residual responsibilities that are better managed centrally, such as the retirement and health benefits systems. The OFM would also assist in selecting key administration officials, such as the assistant secretaries for management, giving more weight to management skills in comparison with technical abilities and political connections. Key OFM officials would be appointed for long periods and have strong management backgrounds.[23]

This approach shares with the designers of the CSRA a desire to delegate as much authority as possible to line managers. It differs in its perspective on reorganization. The CSRA created the OPM as the executive branch's personnel management leader and tried to infuse the OPM with concern for public management and productivity, broadly defined. This was done, in part, to separate the responsibilities for personnel policy leadership from those of adjudication of employee appeals; both formerly had resided in the Civil Service Commission. It was also done in recognition of the close relationship between personnel policy and productivity improvements, and in response to the reality—also observed by the Grace Commission—that the OMB remains preoccupied with the annual budgetary process, largely to the neglect of broader management concerns.

The Grace Commission's recommendation to shift responsibility to a supermanagement agency may spring from a disenchantment with the OPM's performance to date in providing leadership in management. The current director's return to "bedrock personnel management" can be seen as a retreat from the broader role envisioned for the OPM by the designers of the CSRA. Whether the OPM is incapable of providing such leadership, or is simply disinterested at present, is yet to be demonstrated.

In any case, the proposed solution by the Grace Commission is unlikely to be approved in any form that might truly improve management leadership. As Richard P. Nathan, Hugh Heclo, and

22. PPSSCC, *Report on Federal Management Systems*, pp. v–vi.
23. Ibid., p. x.

others have pointed out, there are strong pressures for more, rather than less, political involvement in governmental appointments.[24] For example, it is hard to imagine any modern-day president coexisting with a budget director not of his choosing. If the head of the OFM were appointed for a term extending beyond a change of administration, then the highly political budget process would probably be shifted to some shadow organization more fully under presidential control. Moreover, there is no reason to expect that the head of the OFM would have any greater commitment to management issues than have recent heads of the OMB. The short-term demands of the budget process work to drive out broader attention to management. Based upon past experience with the shift from the Bureau of the Budget to the Office of Management and Budget, merely telling the OFM to be concerned with management issues and not to become preoccupied with the budget process is likely to head off domination of the important by the urgent.

The appeal of coordinating the interrelated functions of budget, planning, and management improvement, by placing them all within one agency, must be evaluated against the argument that the priority of good personnel management can be raised on the government's agenda more effectively by giving responsibility for this issue to a high-level appointee with relatively few competing concerns. That is the model pursued by the CSRA. Its workability is untested, and further reorganization is premature.

Another management initiative proposed by the commission and consistent with the CSRA is to delegate as much authority to line managers as can be justified. For Alan Campbell, the OPM's director during the Carter administration, that meant large-scale delegations of staffing and other authorities, using a liberal interpretation of the statute. For the Grace Commission, the decision to delegate rests on a comparative analysis of cost. Drawing on private sector practice, where "cost-effectiveness is usually the key consideration" in decisions to centralize or decentralize,[25] the commission recommends that the OPM delegate authority to agencies whenever delegation can be cost justified. The proposal to consolidate personnel services, for example, is discussed almost entirely in economies of scale.[26] One difficulty

24. Richard P. Nathan, *The Administrative Presidency* (John Wiley & Sons, 1983); Hugh Heclo, "OMB and the Presidency: The Problem of Neutral Competence," *Public Interest,* vol. 38 (Winter 1975), pp. 80–98.

25. PPSSCC, *Report on Federal Management Systems,* sec. 2, p. 16.

26. PPSSCC, *Report on Personnel Management,* pp. 188–93.

with the commission's preoccupation with cost is that it allows simplistic short-term dollar savings to overshadow attention to long-term program savings from better management, a more difficult benefit to measure.

A more fundamental difficulty is that the Grace Commission does not recognize that centralized control is especially valued in government for reasons that have little to do with cost. Relatively little time to implement desired policy changes, distrust of bureaucrats, and excessive desire to avoid mistakes that are newsworthy make centralized control especially appealing to political appointees in the federal government. The GAO and congressional committee staff encourage the appointees' urge to centralize, since oversight of federal programs is easier when decisions are made centrally.

For example, Donald Devine, Reagan's director of the OPM, interprets the law on delegations more narrowly than did Campbell. With congressional encouragement, Devine has pulled back to the OPM a number of staffing delegations, most notably for filling positions at or above the GS–9 level. Interestingly, the Grace Commission's analysis warns that severe staff cuts at the OPM over the past few years and a loss of many of the most experienced staffing specialists have led to a deterioration in the quality and timeliness of staffing service.[27] Nonetheless, centralizing continues. The number of jobs filled per year at or over GS–9 is relatively small—approximately 500—but each job requires the individual treatment of announcements and examinations. If the OPM supplies slower and less adequate service in filling these positions, the OPM imposes a serious, unquantified cost on agency operations, especially since agencies consider these jobs particularly important to accomplishing their missions.

Both the Grace Commission and the early interpreters of the CSRA favor more extensive delegation of personnel authority to line managers than currently exists. Neither reform approach addresses adequately the resistance to delegation that characterizes federal government operations. The lesson from experience under the CSRA is that wishing for delegation in government will not make it happen. Sustained leadership, committed to as much delegation as possible, is necessary before authority will remain with line managers. Perhaps decentralization in the public sector should proceed agency by agency rather than function by function, so that oversight committees can watch what happens and political

27. Ibid., p. 130.

appointees in the central management agencies can convey to line managers exactly what is expected of them.

A third management proposal offered by the Grace Commission is to establish employee surveys in federal departments and agencies.[28] The federal management systems report describes the usefulness of such feedback mechanisms for managers in the private sector. The commission's exclusive attention to survey feedback from employees follows from the commission's top-down view of management. Managers decide and employees react. In contrast, the CSRA proceeds from an assumption that employees must be involved in designing management systems, such as performance appraisal systems, for them to work well.

Nevertheless, the CSRA stimulated the only recent equivalent in the federal government to employee surveys in business—the Federal Employee Attitude Survey (FEAS), administered by the OPM.[29] Under Campbell, the FEAS was designed not only as a central element in evaluating the civil service reforms but also to provide systematic feedback to agencies on the attitudes of employees toward their jobs and work places. That second purpose led the OPM to design the FEAS to include twenty separate agency samples. The OPM then prepared agency reports that were used by several agencies to stimulate discussion and action to improve employee morale and tighten linkages between job performance and job rewards. The commission and the CSRA, then, share a belief in the desirability of employee feedback mechanisms.

Recent experience with the FEAS, however, highlights the difficulty of conducting such surveys under an administration that considers the results embarrassing to political leaders. The first FEAS was administered in late 1979, and its results became public within four months. Administration of the latest FEAS was delayed for nearly two years beyond its original 1981 schedule, and agency reports are still unavailable over one year later. The utility of such data for agency managers is obviously limited when so much time passes between survey and report. Moreover, FEAS III is markedly deteriorated in professional design compared with previous questionnaires. A number of questions force responses within an unreasonably narrow range on topics about which federal employees are poorly informed at present. For example,

---

28. PPSSCC, *Report on Federal Management Systems*, sec. 9.
29. U.S. Office of Personnel Management (OPM), *Federal Employee Attitudes, Phase 1: Baseline Survey, 1979* (GPO, 1980); and OPM, *Federal Employee Attitudes, Phase 2: Follow-up Survey, 1980* (GPO, 1983).

employees are asked to agree or disagree with the statement "My employee benefits should be comparable to those in the private sector." Few federal employees know the levels of private sector benefits, how these levels vary depending on which firms or governments are included in comparability calculations, or the probable implications of comparability for their own benefit levels.

Beyond problems with its design, FEAS III suffers from serious weaknesses in the quality and credibility of the data analysis and resulting reports. Under Campbell, all FEAS I data were publicly released. The primary releases from FEAS III so far are only a brief preliminary report and an OPM press release entitled "Fed Employees' Morale High, Survey Shows: Say Appraisals Fair, Willing to Change Mix of Benefits."[30] Many conclusions reached in both releases are unsubstantiated by the data presented. Given that the FEAS III conclusions contradict other studies,[31] that the conclusions clearly serve the political interests of OPM Director Donald Devine, and that the full set of data is not available for public scrutiny, skepticism of these OPM products is surely warranted.

Although the problems of management practice in the federal government are real, the solutions are neither obvious nor simple. The CSRA encourages strong OPM leadership in public management, including delegation and employee feedback. Despite the encouragement, the CSRA's gains have been short-lived. By and large, the Grace Commission picks up on the same management themes, but its recommendations show little promise of any greater success. One more shuffle of responsibility for management improvement is unlikely to be constructive, especially when the direction of the shuffle is back to an agency burdened with the continuous demands of budget preparation. Meanwhile, the Grace Commission—just like the CSRA—fails to offer workable suggestions on how to delegate and establish feedback mechanisms in a system under strong pressures to centralize and to politicize survey results.

Strengthening Research, Demonstrations, and Program Evaluation

Besides studies of federal employee opinion, the Grace Commission also promotes systematic research, demonstrations, and evaluation of government programs. This emphasis is most clearly

---

30. OPM, *Federal Employee Attitudes Survey, Phase 3: Preliminary Report* (GPO, 1984); and OPM, *News*, February 7, 1984.

31. *Senior Executive Service*, pp. 167–69, 418–19; and PPSSCC, *Report on Personnel Management*, p. 114.

stated in the federal management systems report, which recommends more rigorous and systematic evaluations of federal programs designed to produce "results-oriented" data.[32] In personnel management, the Grace Commission recommends that ideas on work force planning garnered from the private sector be tried out in a few locations and carefully evaluated before implementing them governmentwide; that a demonstration project study competitive approaches to providing health benefits for federal workers; and that research identify basic skills and competencies required for effective supervision.[33]

The CSRA, too, promotes the systematic study of personnel management approaches and programs. One of its most exciting provisions is a demonstration authority that allows waiving law or regulation, under specific conditions, to demonstrate and evaluate new approaches in personnel management. The navy demonstration project began under that authority.[34] The designers of the CSRA envisioned the OPM as a leader in systematic research, demonstrations, and personnel program evaluation. What recent experience at the OPM demonstrates is the vulnerability of program evaluation and research to the changing priorities of agency heads.

Under Director Alan Campbell, the OPM welcomed new ideas in personnel management and encouraged experimentation and systematic study. The OPM moved aggressively to identify and publicize productivity improvements in the federal government, to serve as a clearinghouse on public management research, to stimulate and monitor demonstration projects, to provide integrated consulting service on personnel issues to departments and agencies, and to evaluate the effectiveness of program changes made under the CSRA. Campbell built staff competence at the OPM in research and evaluation techniques. His staff designed both short- and long-term studies of productivity improvement, CSRA initiatives, and other public management issues. The evaluation of the CSRA governmentwide stimulated the evaluation of personnel management programs in other departments and agencies. There were new efforts to improve communication and cooperation among members of the research community con-

32. PPSSCC, *Report on Federal Management Systems,* p. x and sec. 10.
33. PPSSCC, *Report on Personnel Management,* pp. 57–65, 163–72, 194–99.
34. See "Status of the Evaluation of the Navy Personnel Management Demonstration Project: Management Report" and "Evaluation of the Navy Personnel Management Demonstration Project: Analysis of Survey and Interview Results, 1979–1983, Management Report II" (OPM, 1984).

cerned with improving public management. For example, with OPM leadership, the central management agencies sponsored two conferences on public management research; the OPM developed a newsletter to share information about research activities and findings; and the office held regular meetings to coordinate evaluation efforts to assess the CSRA.[35]

Nearly all of these initiatives have been cut severely under Director Devine, who has led a retreat from program evaluation and systematic research in public management by the OPM. Devine's priorities suggest impatience with investments in systematic research that promise primarily long-term payoffs. Under Devine, the OPM dismantled its productivity and public management research efforts as well as most of its CSRA program evaluation. Aside from the navy demonstration, the OPM devoted little attention during Devine's first three years in office to the CSRA demonstration authority, approving only one small demonstration on alternative training and recruitment practices for technical occupations at the Federal Aviation Administration.[36]

The OPM is being criticized for inadequate leadership in program evaluation. The General Accounting Office criticized the OPM for focusing solely on processes and procedures used in performance appraisal to the nearly total neglect of study of the quality of performance appraisal systems and their effectiveness in meeting public management goals.[37] The GAO also found that only one agency among those visited had conducted a serious evaluation of agency executive development programs.[38]

Perhaps the most vigorous evaluation effort occurred under Devine's attempts to use evaluation for the internal control of government operations, rather than for learning why personnel management practices succeed or fail. However, Devine's approach—to develop report cards on agencies based on questionable quantitative indicators—is likely to be harmful rather than beneficial. First, the OPM's credibility will be suspect if it issues

35. OPM, "Setting Public Management Research Agendas: Integrating the Sponsor, Producer and User," *Proceedings of the Public Management Research Conference* (Washington, D.C., 1979); OPM, "The Changing Character of the Public Work Force," *Proceedings of the Second Public Management Research Conference* (Washington, D.C., 1980); and OPM, *Public Management Research,* a quarterly news update, various issues in 1980 and 1981.

36. OPM, *News,* "OPM Gives Final Approval to FAA Demonstration Project," July 15, 1983; and "Airway Science Curriculum; Approval of Demonstration Project Final Plan," *Federal Register,* vol. 48, no. 137, pp. 32490–32500.

37. GAO, "An Assessment of SES Performance Appraisal Systems" (GAO/GGD-84-16, May 16, 1984), pp. iv–v; 17–20.

38. GAO, "Progress Report on Federal Executive Development Programs" (GAO/GGD-84-92, August 15, 1984), pp. 1–3.

indefensible conclusions based on "number crunching" performed without any serious effort to understand what the numbers truly mean. Second, should the numbers be taken seriously, they will predictably induce goal displacement. Agency people will do what is necessary to look "good" in terms of particular numbers, without any accompanying effort to do a better job overall. Third, Devine's top-down view of how to change bureaucratic practice inevitably will encourage recalcitrance on the part of the data providers. The OPM is choosing an adversarial approach to evaluation, which is less likely to stimulate desirable change than would more cooperative approaches that share information with line managers and discuss ways to improve practice.[39]

Finally, Director Devine has politicized the research and evaluation processes in OPM so completely that outsiders no longer accept OPM reports as professional research products. For example, Devine's subordinate, James Byrnes, suggested in writing how studies of pay equity could be manipulated for partisan political purposes, prompting congressional hearings and contributing to House passage of an amendment that delayed and almost killed prospects for important personnel legislation.[40] By placing the CSRA evaluation program alongside public affairs in a highly partisan Office of Policy and Communications, Devine signaled unmistakably what the role is of research and evaluation in his agency. Since Devine took over, the OPM has lost many of its best employees trained in research and evaluation.

Under Campbell the CSRA temporarily raised the priority of public management research and serious evaluation of personnel management programs. However, that emphasis has not survived the presidential transition. The CSRA provides opportunities for research and evaluation in the personnel management area but no guarantees that serious studies will be done. The Grace Commission's suggestions are equally well meaning, but without commitment to serious research and evaluation in the OPM, these recommendations will make little difference.

Yet, the kinds of large-scale changes in personnel management and productivity that the Grace Commission promotes should be informed by systematic learning about the public sector. At points

39. Gerald Barkdoll, "Type III Evaluation," *Public Administration Review*, vol. 40 (March–April 1980), pp. 174–79.
40. James L. Byrnes's memorandum on the pay equity bill to Director Donald J. Devine, OPM, May 14, 1984; and House Resolutions 2300 and 5680, Civil Service Retirement Spouse Equity Act of 1984, and Federal Pay Equity and Management Improvement Act of 1984.

in its report, the commission seems to forget its own advice. For example, the commission recommends introducing massive changes in the procedures for conducting reductions in force without any prior smaller trials or systematic study. In doing so, the commission urges that greater weight be placed on employee performance when making decisions about reductions in force, even though performance appraisal systems in the federal government are still under development, lack wide acceptance, and obviously are weak at the executive level.[41] The commission also encourages contracting with entities outside government but without simultaneously recommending careful experiments to assess relative cost, quality of service, and accountability of contracted and noncontracted services over time.[42] The commission's concern with improving productivity is obvious, but the report talks of the need for training and seminars without equal stress on needed research and systematic evaluation of techniques to determine the training and instructional approaches that are most effective in particular circumstances.[43]

Federal personnel management occurs within a complex system; changes in the rules in one area often affect the ability to achieve goals elsewhere. Knowledge about what works well in this complex system and how to improve current deficiencies in the public sector is limited. The Grace Commission acknowledges the system's complexity when the commission cautions, for example, that office consolidation could undermine efforts to give line managers in agencies more authority over personnel management actions. Other obvious complexities are not acknowledged by the commission, such as how proposed changes in procedures for reductions in force and benefits levels for senior executives could make federal jobs less attractive and impede recruitment goals. Given our limited knowledge about public sector operations, the complexity of the system is a powerful reason to use research and demonstration capacity to experiment with changes in controlled and limited settings before applying them governmentwide.

Perhaps the limited knowledge of government is what leads so many people to private sector practice and studies for guidance. Yet, public and private situations differ in significant ways. Private businesses and federal installations also vary tremendously in the circumstances they face. Rather than simply assume that private

41. GAO, "An Assessment," pp. i–v.
42. PPSSCC, *Report on Personnel Management,* pp. 152–57.
43. Ibid., pp. 181–87.

business practices will succeed in government, a more prudent approach experiments first on a limited scale and then evaluates the results. Public–private sector differences do exist, with important implications for the likely success of private approaches in federal operations. The federal government should step back and examine these differences and question a central assumption of the Grace Commission—that private business practice can and should be transplanted into federal government operations.

Transplanting private sector practice

The designers of the Civil Service Reform Act of 1978 and the members of the Grace Commission shared an enthusiasm for promoting the use of private sector practices in the federal government to improve government performance. One lesson of the civil service reform experience is that, while public sector managers have a great deal to learn from their counterparts in private industry (and vice versa), efforts to transplant practice from one sector to the other are rarely simple. Significant differences between public and private enterprises affect the way that each one operates. Moreover, so much diversity occurs within both domains that generalizations about either one should be highly suspect.

Assumptions about Private Sector Practice

Important provisions of the CSRA are based on assumptions about the potential similarity of performance measurement in the public and private sectors and the effectiveness in both realms of monetary incentives as motivators of good performance.[44] The CSRA also rests on an assumption that government performance can be improved by approximating the private sector practice of giving top executives control over the selection of their key management team. Once the CSRA was signed into law, the OPM's Director, Campbell, invited private sector specialists in personnel and compensation to assist government agencies in designing and implementing new personnel practices.

The Grace Commission's enchantment with private sector practice is even more intense. The commission was composed of people from the private sector who drew on their own experience, among other things, to generate recommendations for improving public operations. A number of those recommendations use average practice in the private sector as an explicit benchmark for

44. Alan K. Campbell, "A Frame for the Three Faces," *Journal of Policy Analysis and Management,* vol. 2 (Summer 1983), pp. 526–30.

comparative purposes and a goal for the federal government. Such an approach assumes that performance in the private sector is superior to performance in government, that the criteria for measuring performance are substantially the same in both sectors, and that private and public operations are similar enough in most fundamental respects to permit successful procedural transplants from the private sector to the public sector. Yet, there are important distinctions between private and public activity and considerable variety in practice in both domains.

The designers of the CSRA recognized the distinctions and diversity. For example, they wondered whether monetary incentives would prove to be as effective in motivating employees in the government as they have been in private business. They recognized the special political pressures on employees in government and enumerated prohibited personnel practices explicitly in the CSRA. A four-month "cooling off" period is mandated in the CSRA, during which new political appointees may not transfer career senior executives involuntarily. This and other provisions reflect the designers' sensitivity to important differences between government and business environments. Moreover, in recognition of the substantial diversity of circumstances within the federal government, the CSRA permits agencies to design their own performance appraisal system and other personnel systems to suit their particular needs. Just after the law was passed, OPM leaders resisted entreaties from the GAO and elsewhere to provide more stringent guidance to agencies, preferring instead to "let a thousand flowers bloom." Even so, the OPM's leaders can be criticized for underestimating the significance of differences between the public and private sectors, and in particular for underestimating the force of politics on the government reforms they attempted to put in place.

What the CSRA underestimates, the Grace Commission ignores. The Grace Commission report emphasizes neither distinctions between public and private sectors nor diversity within either one. Instead, it glosses over differences between and within sectors. Typical is the following statement from the commission's report on management systems, "Although there are differences in operating styles and requirements between the public and private sectors of our economy . . . we have conducted our study and developed our recommendations on the principle that private sector approaches can help improve managing the Government's business."[45] The assumption of sector similarity is so central to

45. PPSSCC, *Report on Federal Management Systems*, p. ii.

the rationales offered by the Grace Commission for its recommendations that the assumption warrants detailed examination. To the extent that this central assumption is unjustified, a basic foundation of the commission's work begins to crumble.

Similarities and Differences

Over the past several years, quite a bit has been written comparing management in the private and public sectors.[46] Much of it focuses on whether the sectors are more alike or different, a question that contributes little to guiding action. What needs to be understood instead are the differences that do exist and their implications for the workability and desirability of various reform proposals.

One of the most frequently cited distinctions between the private and public sectors is the purported lack of a bottom line in public agencies. Yet, that distinction can easily be overdrawn. Some government functions look and operate much like traditional profit centers in the private sector. Training courses are sold by the OPM to agencies, and the OPM's training centers are held accountable for recovering their costs. Internal Revenue Service agents calculate the probable tax recovered per hour for different types of audits, and agents concentrate their efforts in areas of likely payoff. Some government activities can be compared directly to private business operations. Government workers write checks, process insurance claims, maintain ships and buildings, and run hospitals. While there is no requirement that public agencies show a profit, the Office of Management and Budget guidelines for contracting services with the private sector (when those services can be provided there at lower cost) provide a marketlike approximation.[47] Besides, many employees in the private sector work in staff functions, where there are no more obvious profit and loss considerations than in similar government functions. Therefore, while some public employees are engaged in work very different from what is done in the private sector, large numbers of public employees occupy jobs very similar to those

46. Graham T. Allison, Jr., "Public and Private Management: Are They Fundamentally Alike in All Unimportant Respects?" in OPM, "Setting Public Management Research Agendas: Integrating the Sponsor, Producer and User," pp. 27–38; Hal G. Rainey, Robert W. Backoff, and Charles H. Levine, "Comparing Public and Private Organizations," *Public Administration Review,* vol. 36 (March–April 1976); and Michael Blumenthal, "Candid Reflections of a Businessman in Washington," *Fortune,* January 29, 1979.

47. U.S. Office of Management and Budget, Circular A-76, especially the revision of April 5, 1979.

of private sector workers. Some agencies are more similar to the private sector than others, and private sector approaches are most relevant for them.

Of broader significance are differences in the fundamental purposes and the political environments of public and private sector organizations. Besides operating many quasi businesses efficiently, government is also expected to protect citizens' liberties and to pursue other goals—such as equality—that American citizens value.[48] That does not mean that efficiency is unimportant in the government but that efficiency is only one of the goals of government service, not its primary goal. Unable to be single-minded in pursuing efficiency, the government will rarely be—and is not intended to be—as efficient as is business.

In order to protect this country from the arbitrary use of power, those who crafted the Constitution intentionally designed a system in which power is separated and widely shared. As a consequence, decisionmaking processes in the government are much more chaotic and complex than in the business world. With less orderly decisionmaking than the typical private sector operation, government organizations may require different mixes of resources to accomplish the same tasks.

Moreover, the framers of the Constitution never anticipated the large and diverse civil service that exists today, and they provided no explicit guidance on the proper place of the bureaucracy in the political system. The design of the American political system makes the complete, businesslike subordination of executive departments to the president virtually impossible. Constitutional design, coupled with a multiplicity of interests in the country, guarantees that the interests of the White House, an agency's political leadership, and members of Congress rarely converge. With a constitutionally based fuzzing of hierarchical control in the public sector, and contradictory orders coming from various legitimate sources, the job of the public manager is especially challenging. Those who focus on the similarities of the public and private sectors tend to have an image of a civil service that is hierarchically subordinate to, and solely responsive to, the president and his priorities. That image is unrealistic given the structure and design of this country's government.

The multiple masters of the federal bureaucracy do not speak with one voice about which value should receive highest priority in government policies and programs. What results is constant

48. Arthur M. Okun, *Equality and Efficiency: The Big Tradeoff* (Brookings, 1975).

tension in the system among the ideal arrangements for maximizing efficiency and those which are ideal for maximizing other values. The difficulty of pursuing important values simultaneously stimulates the cyclical nature of much of personnel reform. First the system is centralized to improve efficiency, and then it is decentralized to improve responsiveness. Or, first the system is regulated to promote equity, and then it is deregulated to promote efficiency. The constant churning of organizational structures and functions in government agencies is a natural outgrowth of the system's design, which impedes efficient performance by public managers.

In addition, performance in the public sector is more difficult to achieve than in business organizations because of the greater scrutiny of public activities by outsiders, including the media and Congress. At the top, nearly every government agency is subjected to more publicity, investigation, and interference than is typical of private sector organizations. Unusual ancedotes sustain public scrutiny; cases that may be out of the ordinary become cause célèbres. Such scrutiny is hardly neutral in focus or effect. Mistakes and problems are usually more newsworthy than are smooth operations and successes. In contrast, business leaders are permitted some mistakes, in part because they operate largely out of public view. They can keep their attention riveted on broader goals, while their public sector counterparts watch an entire program unravel because of the publicity given to a single mistake.

The time and energy required of federal executives to defend and explain their programs can be considerable. They appear before Congress; they meet with staff from the General Accounting Office and the Office of Management and Budget; and they field questions from the media. Few would argue seriously for government in private, although many might yearn for less scrutiny and more balanced news coverage than is common. To keep programs moving efficiently in the midst of heightened visibility and criticism requires substantial executive resources.

Finally, there is no wholesale change in leadership in most businesses as there is in government. Political appointees stay on the job and in their government agencies only a short time. Private sector managers move but usually within the company and not in and out of a "government of strangers."[49] The personal networks that facilitate cooperative action in business are largely absent in the top echelons of government leadership. Frequent turnover at

49. Hugh Heclo, *A Government of Strangers: Executive Politics in Washington* (Brookings, 1977).

the top makes many of the Grace Commission's recommendations especially difficult to achieve.

The demands of executive jobs in the public and private sectors are different. As a consequence of the special characteristics of government organizations and their environments, higher numbers of supervisors and staff positions are predictable in federal service than would be necessary or desirable in the private sector. Management arrangements in the government must, and should, reflect the multiple legitimate goals of public activity rather than single out only one goal—efficiency—and elevate its status relative to others. These significant realities should condition any recommendations for change.

Government Diversity

Beyond these important differences between public and private organizations, which limit the usefulness of the Grace Commission's recommendations, is the wide variety of activities, environments, and practices that exists in government agencies. With so much diversity, proposals to apply averages from the private sector to the public sector are almost meaningless.

For example, the Grace Commission estimates the average ratio of supervisors to subordinates in the private sector and then urges the public sector to conform to that average.[50] Such an approach ignores several important realities. First, the private sector estimate of average practice is only approximate, based inevitably upon skewed samples of business firms that often provide data of questionable validity. Second, the private sector is not appropriately viewed as a monolith. An appropriate supervisor-to-subordinate ratio for a hospital is likely to be inappropriate for a management consulting firm. Utilizing a mathematical average is tidy but simplistic; it ignores the incomparabilities of specific firms. Third, the diversity in federal government organizations also makes attention to averages simplistic. Fourth, an average or range for business may not be appropriate for government. Although it is true that the distributions of public and private sector circumstances overlap, the distributions are not identical, and the extreme cases in each sector require special consideration.

Finally, it is notable that students of the private sector are highly

---

50. Grace, *War on Waste,* pp. 231–32. In its own report on supervisor-to-subordinate ratios, the GAO found broader spans of control in the public sector than in the private sector. GAO also cautioned against the use of aggregate data to compare government and business. See GAO, "Supervisory to Nonsupervisory Ratios in the Public and Private Sectors" (FPCD-80-65, September 30, 1980).

critical of the present state of personnel management there as well.[51] Neither sector has a monopoly on good or poor management practice. Each obviously benefits from looking at the very best that the other has to offer, so long as that look is taken with the realization that adjustments are often needed before transplants can succeed.

Conclusions

Experience over the past six years under the 1978 civil service reforms suggests certain caveats regarding the practicality and desirability of the Grace Commission's recommendations. First, changing personnel management in the federal government takes time and requires sustained leadership in a consistent direction. When political leadership changes frequently, reforms are often judged prematurely and sometimes reversed before they have had enough time to work. For example, a proposal to shift responsibility for leadership in personnel management and productivity from the Office of Personnel Management to the Office of Federal Management is premature and derives from a faulty belief that structural changes and procedural requirements are enough to create management excellence. Understanding how reform succeeds or why reform fails takes time, patience, and study.

Second, promoting unrealistic expectations about the financial gains to flow from policy changes threatens employees' morale and trust. The difficulties of forging a legislative coalition to pass new laws often encourage exaggeration and unwarranted optimism in promises about what the laws will accomplish. In federal personnel policy, such hyperbole fosters expectations by employees and the public that will be unmet. The disappointment and resulting cynicism colors the current landscape, now magnifying the challenges for federal personnel management reforms.

Third, calculating benefit-cost ratios for personnel management programs in the public sector is complex. It requires the incorporation of benefits and costs related to the multiple goals of public action, and it requires attention to both long- and short-term consequences. Most of the benefits and costs are not easily quantified. Without vigilance, short-term and direct dollar savings will assume more importance than is warranted, relative to long-term indirect savings and to long-term costs in program equity, government responsiveness, and individual liberty.

Finally, systematic experimentation and study are essential

51. One of the latest is Daniel Yankelovich and John Immerwahr, *Putting the Work Ethic to Work* (New York: The Public Agenda Foundation, 1983).

before massive changes are introduced governmentwide. That principle is written into law in the CSRA, and its importance is acknowledged by the Grace Commission report. Nonetheless, the CSRA demonstration authority is underutilized, and evaluation of personnel management programs is underemphasized. The impatience of short-term politicians—anxious for immediate, visible change—makes investment in systematic study unpopular. But the complexity of management in the public sector and the diversity of its circumstances demand deliberateness in establishing a foundation for governmentwide change.

In summary, there are no shortcuts to effective reform in federal personnel management. Transplants from the private sector are worth considering but only after adjusting them appropriately for public purposes.

General Discussion

HOWARD MESSNER, assistant administrator for administration and resources management, the Environmental Protection Agency, led the discussion by saying that in twenty-six years of federal service he has learned that the management of the federal government cannot be improved or maintained without the involvement of the employees. The definition of the problem occupies so many people who come from the outside, that the time involved in defining the problem usually ends up replacing the time involved in working out the problem.

Messner reflected on his experience of working with J. Peter Grace at the beginning of the commission's work. Messner said that Grace approached the issue of defining the problem of federal management as a cost question; he was predisposed to believe that the federal government is more expensive than it should be. Grace's earliest questions involved how to save money, not whether money is there to be saved. In contrast, Alan Campbell and the framers of the civil service Reform Act approached the issue by considering how to motivate the work force to be more imaginative, stimulating, and thoughtful. Cost savings were considered a by-product of workers' satisfaction. Messner said that it is important to recognize that both reform initiatives started with a negative image of the civil service work force.

Messner addressed some gaps in the Grace Commission's report that he said were also overlooked by the Civil Service Reform Act (CSRA). For example, there is a real underestimation of the role of the political process in management, and this is what distinguishes management in the public sector from that in the private sector. Differences like sunshine legislation in the public sector take a long time for private sector executives to understand when they come into the government. In the public sector, criticism by executives of one another is part of the rules of the game, but such criticism is rare in business. Business managers prove themselves on standards of profitability, while the public service must use other measures of performance.

95

James S. Cowan, special counsel to the Senate Subcommittee on Civil Service, Post Office, and General Services, commented that it is easy for business executives to say that the government should be run like a business, not realizing that there are some significant differences between the private and public sectors. For example, he said, the commission's proposal that the Senior Executive Service (SES) be made smaller is probably correct but not necessarily for the reasons that the commission gave. Part of the problem with the SES is that many of the positions are highly technical, and there cannot be much mobility between jobs. Many of the SES positions probably should not be in the SES; indeed, some should be paid higher salaries. Cowan said that the SES should be reserved for managers who can be as fungible as possible. While not sure of what the number would be, he thought that 1,500 is probably a rather drastically small number.

Cowan said that the recommendation about separating executive pay and congressional pay is impossible to accomplish as long as Congress has to unwillingly decide its own pay year after year. Cowan pointed to legislation passed the previous week that increases the amount of money available for bonuses and removes the pay cap on bonuses above executive level I salaries. He said that the big problem with bonuses is exacerbated by the publicity about bonuses that prompts Congress to crack down on bonus arrangements. Cowan hopes that the Office of Personnel Management (OPM) will control the bonus system better in the future, because deterioration of the bonus program would be unfortunate for the federal government.

Cowan thought the commission's recommendation for an Office of Federal Management was useless. He thought it duplicated the functions of the Office of Personnel Management. He said the OPM should broaden its horizons to be the place where emphasis on improving management in the federal government resides.

As far as delegation of authority for personnel management to the agencies was concerned, Cowan said that his committee had supported the OPM's recentralization of authority because it was easier for Congress to exercise oversight in this area. Cowan added that the committee wholeheartedly agreed that demonstration projects, within the terms of the CSRA, were a good idea. In fact, he said, most of the major changes in the CSRA should have been demonstrated first. In general, Congress favors an increase in the demonstration project authority, and he hoped that the administration would take the lead in facilitating those projects.

Finally, Cowan said that he thought the most serious drawback in the Grace Commission's recommendations was its emphasis on dollar savings and not management improvement. He said that is partly why the Grace Commission has not been well received by congressional committees. It is difficult for Congress— at least the relevant committees—to take those recommendations seriously when the commission was supposed to concentrate on management improvement and instead highlighted budgeting issues that have been discussed for many years. In closing, Cowan said that it was his understanding that the commission was prohibited from talking to congressional staff and congressional committees. By excluding Congress, the commission pretty much dug its own grave.

David Stanley asked Goldenberg and Messner about the need for improved communications among employees in the federal government, particularly as it affects labor relations.

Goldenberg responded that during 1979 and 1980, the Office of Personnel Management made good use of the Federal Employee Attitudes Survey to get direct feedback from employees and to encourage faster implementation of performance appraisal systems. To be useful, such surveys must be timely and credible. The most recent employee survey was delayed for two years and, consequently, the data are not useful or credible.

Messner said that polling data have a modest role to play in employee communication. He added that there is a difference between employee communication that is defensive and aimed at protecting some benefits, and employee participation in management. He said a more promising direction was the discussions between the administration and groups like the Public Employee Roundtable and the Senior Executive Association. In those discussions, participants seek to set aside contentious issues in which they have a vested interest and instead talk about improving management and achieving excellence in government. Messner thinks that some real initiatives and interest among employees in productivity improvement are starting to occur.

William Colman, director of research, National Committee on Public Employee Pensions, said that the idea of strengthening the OPM's management role instead of creating a new overall Office of Federal Management has a lot of merit but would entail removing the "M" from the OMB and putting it into the OPM. He asked if this proposal would broaden the mission of the OPM to embrace general management and wondered if this would require an amendment to the CSRA.

Cowan answered no, as long as such a change didn't involve procurement, since procurement authority obviously is a function of the General Services Administration. But if one is talking only about the functions that the OMB exercises in management, much of that work is redundant with what the OPM does.

Goldenberg added that the OPM could broaden its sights without taking in the whole domain of management. The OPM is capable of working cooperatively with the OMB. She did not think that every new administration has to make structural changes to improve management. She said that it takes time to see things improve and work out; a little patience with the current structural design is needed to see what can be accomplished before trying to change it again.

Patrick Korten then focused the discussion on the demonstration projects. He said the OPM had not undertaken more experiments because it had difficulties making performance appraisals and merit raises work well. He cited the navy's China Lake experiment as a demonstration that has worked well. Although the OPM has received scores of proposals for demonstration projects, he said that very few of them had much merit. He mentioned an interagency working group that had been considering other ideas for the past six or eight months. In addition, the OPM is considering a number of ideas in performance management, which is probably the most important single field for the OPM right now.

Korten added that the OPM is becoming more active in demonstration projects. Korten said that he and Director Devine were not satisfied with the quality of the Federal Employee Attitude Survey. The study will be released soon but has been available internally at the OPM for several months. He said that the OPM was also trying to encourage more cooperative than confrontational relationships in the labor relations field by studying and instituting arrangements for constructive consultation with employee organizations.

Goldenberg disagreed with Korten about the quality of the demonstration proposals considered by the OPM. She said that although there aren't a lot of well-thought-out proposals and well-conceived ideas floating around that require waiver of law and regulation, the demonstration provisions of the CSRA did provide a reputation that feasible ideas were welcome at the OPM, which generated a lot of ideas that did not require waiver of law and regulation.

John Golden, director of personnel, Department of Commerce,

said that the thinking of the senior personnel core of the federal government was generally overlooked in deliberations about improving the system. Golden said that he disagreed with the assertions that nothing good is happening; there are a lot of good things going on in the system. He observed that many political leaders are interested in strong and good management and allow personnel directors an opportunity to develop good personnel systems in their departments and agencies. He said that more thought should be given to tapping the experience of personnel specialists in trying to resolve the problems that have been identified.

Eugene McGregor asked if Golden would elaborate on his remarks about how the experience of senior personnel executives might benefit government management.

Golden responded that he, for example, was involved in Reform 88 issues and had developed a proposal for the OMB about correcting overclassification. He mentioned a program on performance management currently working at the Department of Commerce and a paperwork reduction program for personnel actions as examples of good ideas being implemented by individual departments and agencies. Those ideas could be used to improve the personnel system governmentwide. Golden said the central issue is the size of problems; there are few large management problems in government; there are piles of small problems that can be solved one at a time. An example is morale. No one single thing can be done to improve morale in the federal government, but lots of small things can be done within the framework of an overall strategy.

Dennis Little, director of research, Merit Systems Protection Board, mentioned a soon-to-be-released study on the Senior Executive Service. The study found that, regarding compensation, current SES members felt that their contract in essense had been broken. When asked why they stayed and what their incentive was to work, Little said the executives felt they could contribute importantly to policymaking. The survey also found that massive changes in the retirement system and adverse public opinion about federal employees would cause many SES members to leave federal service. Finally, different agencies have different perspectives about the efficacy of the SES provisions of the CSRA.

Little then asked Cowan whether he was advocating a two-tier senior executive system—one for scientists and technologists and one for senior managers.

Cowan responded, "not necessarily." He said that currently in supergrade positions some people are not really senior executives, they are technicians. He felt that the SES currently holds too many technical positions, and some of these people ought to be brought back to supergrades (GS–16 to GS–18). He advised that some incentives—maybe special pay—be awarded to those technicians, so that their opportunity for compensation is not impaired.

Craig Cumbey, director of civilian personnel, U.S. Air Force, said that currently many positions in the SES are scientific and technical jobs. His agency has had trouble getting new appointments made to the SES because many of these people are not clearly managerial. If a separate pay system could be established for that category of people, it would simultaneously reduce the size of the SES and make recruitment of new people easier without causing any great trauma to the people who are in the SES already.

Charles Levine asked Korten if the OPM is capable of accepting all the personnel management responsibility that the Grace Commission has proposed for an Office of Federal Management, assuming such an office is not created.

Korten answered that he preferred not to talk about the Office of Federal Management because it is the only proposal of the Grace Commission that the OPM disagrees with. He said it would introduce a large operational responsibility into the Executive Office of the President, and that responsibility should not be there. Personnel management activities should take place at the OPM.

Korten added that the OPM and the OMB have developed a good working division of labor that allows the OPM to be specific on issues of personnel management. But, Korten said, he would hesitate to draw to the OPM all the functions and authorities of the proposed Office of Federal Management. He reminded the conference that the OPM, as an agency responsible directly to the president, is only six years old and is still finding its way in relationships with the other central management agencies.

Ronald Moe said there were some mistaken views about what was meant by the concept of management. He said that more concern about the general management laws that cut across all of government is needed. Moe said that the OMB, the central management agency of the government, has lost its institutional capacity to answer fundamental questions concerning cross-cutting management issues. He proposed that a fairly small Office of Federal Management could tackle those issues. Such an office would not handle personnel issues; it would be on an equal plane with the OMB and have access to the president.

Tom Diaz, reporter for the *Washington Times,* observed that no one at the conference seemed to be focusing on the question of who is going to pay for such changes, that is, the taxpayer. Better evaluation of the cost of the present system should be a central concern. He said that the subject of cost seems to have been treated as if it were irrelevant.

Responding to Diaz, Cowan said that the way to reduce the costs of government is not to attack the personnel management systems but to reduce government programs. Evaluators can't look at a personnel management system that is not doing particularly well and say the way to cut costs is to cut benefits.

The compensation systems in the government need serious review, but that doesn't mean that substantial changes or costs should come into play. The focus needs to be redefined when cost cutting is the issue.

Armbrust observed that big dollars are at stake in discussions of personnel compensation, but other types of costs, resulting from managerial action, are longer term and are less obvious. A lack of data inhibits a good grasp of the magnitude or scope of some of these important intangibles.

Colman added that one quantitative example of large cost elements in the personnel system is the so-called kicker that was added to the retirement system for the period 1969 to 1976. That cost $38 billion. So there are big ticket items in the personnel field. He said that all dollar parts of the existing personnel systems should not be considered sacrosanct.

Murray Comarow said that some people are defining costs in a very direct and perhaps overly narrow way. The costs of the retirement system are important. But there are other costs that are difficult to quantify but also important such as motivation, morale, training, executive development, and managerial competence. Such costs have direct and powerful bearing upon the costs of running a program or system.

Civil Service Reform: Are the Constraints Impenetrable?

BERNARD ROSEN

DURING THE more than 100-year existence of the federal civil service system, many innovations in personnel policy aimed at building a competent and responsive work force have occurred. The fundamental concept of open competitive examinations introduced in the Civil Service Act of 1883 was followed by laws concerning job classification, pay, retirement, vacation and sick benefits, performance appraisal, training, incentive awards, discipline, and reductions in force. Every statute in these and other areas has been amended, often more than once, to meet new or previously unrecognized problems. None of these personnel policies was established easily or quickly.

Now, in the report prepared by the task force on personnel management of the President's Private Sector Survey on Cost Control, better known as the Grace Commission, recommendations are made for additional changes. It is not surprising that the legislative proposals to reduce employee benefits have generated significant opposition. In this essay I will discuss four constraints on making statutory changes in basic policies governing the federal civil service. Normally, none of these constraints is impenetrable. However, as J. Peter Grace and his associates have demonstrated, the wrong strategy could transform a general constraint into an impenetrable barrier.

The likelihood of adopting good recommendations is enhanced if those seeking to make changes understand at least these potential constraints: political reality, credibility of the reform effort, legal requirements, and administrative uncertainty. The first two are of transcending importance, and they will be examined in greater detail. In discussing these constraints, I will focus on the Grace Commission's shortcomings in order to help us decide what needs to be done now to facilitate favorable consideration of those recommendations that merit adoption.

Political reality

The overriding political reality is that a political process created the civil service system, and therefore significant reforms of the

102

system can be achieved only through that process. Unfortunately, the members and key staff of the authorization committee, in this case the House Post Office and Civil Service Committee, were kept in the dark by the Grace Commission about the issues being explored even though the commission's work would probably result in proposals requiring legislative action. Chairman William Ford expressed unhappiness with this state of affairs in his opening statement at a hearing he conducted on May 24, 1983:

> From the very outset of its inquiry, this subcommittee has encountered difficulty in prying even the most routine information from the survey's executives. The work of these people has been shrouded in secrecy, perhaps to the detriment of the many civic-minded corporate officials who served on the various task forces.
>
> For the record, I feel compelled to say that never in more than 18 years in Congress have I encountered such mystery concerning a presidential blue ribbon panel ostensibly pursuing legitimate objectives.[1]

Chairman Ford's news release on the Grace report on personnel management also made secrecy an issue: "This report is a deceitful attempt to heap more discredit on federal workers by blatantly exaggerating their pay and benefits and by recklessly bending fact as far as proposed savings are concerned—statistical chicanery—in order to produce a document this distorted and biased, the need for secrecy was paramount."[2] The action about which Chairman Ford complained was not simply an oversight. Keeping the agenda and approach secret and locking out the committee and staff were deliberate.

Other organizations whose members have an important stake in the issues considered were treated in the same way. With one limited exception, those organizations too were locked out of the process. There was no consultation on the retirement issue with the National Association of Retired Federal Employees, which has 500,000 members, or the various unions that represent over 1.5 million federal employees. Federal employee unions also have a strong interest in other personnel management subjects explored by the Grace Commission such as pay, health insurance, and contracting out; but they were not consulted on any of these topics. Only in the study of reduction in force did the task force on personnel management seek limited input from unions.

1. Report of the Task Force on Personnel Management of the President's Private Sector Survey on Cost Control, Hearing before the Subcommittee on Investigations of the House Committee on Post Office and Civil Service, 98 Cong. 1 sess. (Government Printing Office, 1983), pp. 57–70.
2. News release, House Post Office and Civil Service Committee, April 14, 1983.

Perhaps the Grace Commission assumed these organizations had nothing useful to contribute. It is true that for many years, only postal employee unions had significant political muscle; but that is no longer true. For example, in 1980 the National Association of Retired Federal Employees raised only $6,000 for political action. But in the first nine months of 1984, it raised more than $1 million from its members. The money is being distributed to support the campaigns for Congress of 182 Democratic candidates and 28 Republican candidates.

In the twenty-two-month period (January 1983–October 1984), fourteen federal employee organizations raised almost $5 million for political action purposes, and most of it was distributed to candidates for Congress. These organizations have members in almost every congressional district. Local chapters hold regular meetings to discuss subjects of high interest. Members hear directly from their union headquarters about issues that affect them. They are urged to act.

The following quotation is from the president of the National Federation of Federal Employees, published in the organization's monthly news magazine shortly after the Grace Commission report on personnel management was released: "As you can learn from the article on the facing page, Mr. Grace's report to the President is riddled with half truths, exaggerations and misstatements that cannot be sustained. Grace has cut at the credibility of federal employee pay and benefits." The article to which the federation president referred highlighted the cost reduction recommendations in the reports and called on every member of the organization to take specified actions to "rebut Grace's twisted facts" with the "facts and figures on this page from several authoritative sources."[3]

Another organization, the American Federation of Government Employees, characterized the Grace Commission report as a "blueprint for disaster."[4] It sharply criticized numerous recommendations and devised a strategy for local chapters and members to follow to defeat the proposals in Congress. Again and again employee organizations are calling on their members to let their representatives and senators know that the recommendations of the Grace Commission to reduce health care, leave, and retirement benefits are unfair and unjustified.

The Grace Commission may have doubted that organizations

3. The remarks appeared in *The Federal Employee,* vol. 69 (February 1984).
4. *The Government Standard,* no. 7 (August 1984), p. 4.

representing employees and retirees possessed any facts and insights useful in a wide-ranging study of the federal civil service, but there is no doubt that the leaders of these organizations disagree. They intend to influence the action taken on the recommendations. They represent more than 2 million employees and retirees and possess effective means for communicating with their members. Excluding them during the process of finding facts and developing proposals invited suspicion and hostility. At best, it indicated a gross insensitivity to political realities; at worst, it projected an image of arrogance and disrespect for democratic decisionmaking. In any event, the exclusionary approach appears to have set back the effort to achieve change.

Credibility of the reform effort

Achieving change through the political process depends greatly on the credibility of the reformers as well as the process. A central issue is whether the overall effort to bring about legislative changes is perceived by decisionmakers and those who may be affected by the recommendations as being in the public interest and conducted responsibly. Credibility depends heavily on the answers to the following questions: Are the objectives of the undertaking clear and in harmony with fundamental needs and values of society? Are those conducting the study professionally competent? Is the publicity initiated or stimulated by those in charge of the reform effort in keeping with the facts? It seems to me that the credibility of the Grace Commission suffers in all three areas: there was and is confusion over objectives; there was a lack of first-rate performance in developing relevant data; and there is significant misinformation being generated in promoting the recommendations.

As for the objectives, there is no question that cost control in the context of increasing efficiency and reducing waste is in the public interest. However, controversy continues over whether the study was supposed to focus on operations, on policy, or on both. The executive order establishing the Private Sector Survey on Cost Control provided this charter for the executive committee:

> (b) The committee shall conduct in-depth reviews of the operations of the executive agencies as a basis for evaluating potential improvements in agency operations.
> (c) In fulfilling its functions the committee shall consider providing recommendations in the following areas: (1) Opportunities for increased efficiency and reduced costs in the federal government that can be realized by executive action or legislation; (2) Areas where managerial accountability can be enhanced and administrative control

can be improved; (3) Opportunities for managerial improvements over both the short and long term; (4) Specific areas where further study can be justified by potential savings; and (5) Information and data relating to governmental expenditures, indebtedness, and personnel management.[5]

Early statements from the White House emphasized that the focus would be on operations. A memorandum from the Office of Management and Budget (OMB) to the assistant secretaries for management described the purpose of the Private Sector Survey on Cost Control. "Its objective is to identify opportunities to (1) eliminate operational overlap and duplication and nonessential administrative activities, and (2) increase management effectiveness in the individual departments and agencies. . . . It will focus on the management processes in contrast to policy and program considerations that result in costly or inefficient activities in the government."[6]

Despite these statements, a joint study by the Congressional Budget Office and the General Acccounting Office determined that over 95 percent of the $424.4 billion savings estimated by the Grace Commission is based on proposed changes in public policy. Selling federally generated electric power at market rather than cost-recovery rates to save $4.5 billion is a public policy question. Limiting growth in medicare and medicaid payments to the annual change in gross national product to save $30 billion is a public policy change. Further reducing food stamps and child nutrition benefits to save $3 billion is a public policy question. The chairman of the House Post Office and Civil Service Committee also concluded that most of the alleged big savings in personnel management are based on policy recommendations. The confusion over objectives has generated controversy about whether the Grace Commission exceeded the publicly stated purpose of its charter, tarnishing the credibility of the effort.

As for the second problem in credibility, the lack of first-rate performance in developing relevant data, the responsible corporate positions held by the participants would lead to an assumption that they possessed the necessary expertise, and I do not question that assumption. Nevertheless, the inadequate justifications for some conclusions and recommendations with the largest projected savings demonstrate unacceptable performance. Consequently, the credibility of the whole effort is undermined.

5. Executive Order 12369 of June 30, 1982.

6. Memorandum from Joseph Wright, deputy director designate, U.S. Office of Management and Budget, to assistant secretaries for management, April 5, 1982.

Total claimed savings are grossly exaggerated. The commission's report contains 2,478 recommendations and claims $424.4 billion would be saved over three years if fully implemented. At the request of the House and Senate Budget Committees, the nonpartisan and highly respected Congressional Budget Office (CBO) and General Accounting Office (GAO) reviewed recommendations accounting for 90 percent of the estimated savings, and, without regard to the merits of the recommendations, they concluded that the savings would be less than one-third of that projected by the Grace Commission.

The conclusion in the CBO–GAO report that many of the Grace Commission's proposals were so vague or unsupported that it was not possible to develop budget estimates also contributes to the credibility gap. The Grace Commission did include a caveat in its report to the effect that some of its figures are useful for planning rather than budgetary purposes; nevertheless, these numbers were used to arrive at the claimed $424.4 billion estimated savings.[7] The letter transmitting the report from J. Peter Grace to the president contained no such caveat; instead it included the widely quoted claim that "These Reports substantiate three-year ongoing savings of $424.4 billion. . . . These are all analyzed and supported in great detail."[8]

Finally, the public information campaign accompanying the Grace Commission's work has shown a disturbing disregard for accuracy. Grossly incorrect data are used to support the campaign to reduce the benefits of federal employees. The greatest claimed savings in personnel management would result from the recommendations to redesign the retirement system. The public has been misled by the allegation that the federal government's civilian employees "retire typically at age 55 versus 63 to 64 in the private sector."[9] The facts are very different. The average age of retirement for federal workers over a recent ten-year period (1973–82) was 61.1. For private sector workers in large companies, average retirement age was 61.8; thus the difference is 0.7 of a year, not 8 or 9 years.[10]

7. U.S. Congressional Budget Office (CBO) and U.S. General Accounting Office (GAO), *Analysis of the Grace Commission's Major Proposals for Cost Control* (GPO, 1984), pp. 1–7.

8. Letter from J. Peter Grace to President Reagan, January 12, 1984.

9. Ibid.

10. Unpublished data on federal workers in the GAO's response to questions from House Post Office and Civil Service Committee, received by the author in 1984; data on private sector workers developed by Johnson and Higgins, consultants, from survey of seventy-two large companies, 1979.

The letter of transmittal from Grace to the president and the public relations campaign that followed allege that the three-year $15.9 billion reduction in benefits would be achieved by only "modifying major federal pensions to provide benefits comparable to those of the best private sector plans." In a May 4, 1984, appearance on the television program *Wall Street Week,* Grace stated that "civil service employees are pensioned at three times the level of generosity as in the Fortune 500. We have a thousand-page study proving that four ways from Sunday." However, the facts are sharply different. At the request of a congressional committee, the GAO studied the pension plan of the W. R. Grace Company, which is quite similar to that of many other large companies. The GAO study shows that for two-thirds of the civil service retirees, the retirement benefits for comparable years of service and salaries are lower, not higher, than those covered by the company plan. Only employees retiring between the ages of fifty-five and fifty-nine with thirty years of service, about one-third of the civil service retirees, enjoy higher benefits under the civil service plan.[11]

Referring to the Grace Commission's conclusion that there is a large gap between federal and private sector retirement practices, the CBO–GAO study stated that "because the PPSSCC proposals to change CSR [civil service retirement] do not include all three types of retirement income found in the private sector (pension plan, Social Security, and capital accumulation plan), GAO does not endorse the PPSSCC recommendations as being based on representative private-sector practices or as sound personnel policy for federal employees."[12]

At the request of the Senate Subcommittee on Civil Service, the GAO is making detailed studies of private sector pension plans. As this is being written, two of the studies have been completed. Several highlights from the published studies help explain the credibility problem of the Grace Commission and why those who would be adversely affected by some recommendations have reacted vehemently with the charge that the report, news releases, and other statements of the Grace Commission are grossly misleading.

One report from the GAO provides information on the prevailing features of private sector retirement programs.[13] This

11. The Comptroller General of the United States, "Comparisons of Retirement Benefits for W. R. Grace and Company and Civil Service Employees" (GAO/OCG-84-1, June 12, 1984), p. 10.

12. CBO and GAO, *Analysis of the Grace Commission's Major Proposals,* p. 262.

13. U.S. General Accounting Office, "Features of Non-federal Retirement Programs" (GAO/OCG-84-2, June 26, 1984).

report deals with features of retirement programs, not levels of benefits. Compared with the federal employee retirement program, some features appear less beneficial to private sector employees and others appear more beneficial. The following are the most significant. First, several features are less beneficial to employees in the private sector:

—Most private plans use the high five-year average salary as the basis for computing benefits, whereas the federal government uses the high three.

—Generally, company plans do not index for inflation, although most employers do provide some inflation adjustments after retirement. The average of such adjustments has been 38 percent of the Consumer Price Index (CPI). Larger employers, those with over 10,000 employees, average 57 percent of the CPI. Annuities of federal employees are fully indexed.

—Retirement at age fifty-five is generally permissible in the private sector, but it is viewed as early retirement and benefits are reduced; whereas in the federal government there is no reduction in benefits provided the employee has thirty years of service. Most private sector plans provide for unreduced benefits at age sixty-two.

Three features stand out as more beneficial to employees in the private sector.

—Contrary to federal practice, very few of the company plans require employee contributions to the pension plan other than for social security. The federal retirement system requires employees to contribute 7 percent of their salaries.

—Most company plans also offer a capital accumulation plan. These take many forms, including employee stock ownership, profit sharing, savings and investment, and deferred compensation plans. Generally, employers match 50 percent or more of the employee contributions, and often both are tax sheltered during preretirement years. There are no such capital accumulation plans for federal employees.

—Private sector plans are coordinated or integrated with social security, which is fully indexed for inflation (also largely exempt from taxes).

Although it is useful to be aware of these major differences, the most important consideration for the employer and employee, private and public, is costs and benefits. Another completed GAO report, which compares the retirement benefits for employees of W. R. Grace and Company with those under the civil service retirement system (CSRS), sheds some light. (Officials of W. R. Grace and Company were asked by the GAO to review the draft of this report. They did so and agreed with both the methodology and the data.[14])

The Grace Company retirement plan consists of a pension plan to which employees do not contribute; a savings plan that permits employees to make pretax contributions of up to 6 percent of pay, which are matched 50 percent by employer contributions; and social security. Grace employees may retire at age fifty-five after any period of service, but if they retire before age sixty-two, the annuity is reduced. Benefits are based on the highest five years.

The GAO made the following four comparisons to evaluate the relative currently authorized retirement benefits of the Grace Company and the federal civil service:

—Grace employee retiring at age sixty-three with seventeen years of service and a final average salary (high five) of $29,441 compared with federal civil service employee retiring at the same age with the same years of service and the same salary history;

—Grace employee retiring at age sixty-three with twenty-four years of service and a final average salary (high five) of $32,438 compared with federal government employee retiring at the same age with the same years of service and salary history;

—Civil service employee retiring at age sixty-one with twenty-nine years of service and a final average salary (high three) of $24,779 compared with Grace employee retiring at the same age with the same years of service and salary history; and

—Civil service employee retiring at age fifty-six with thirty-four years of service and a final average salary (high three) of $25,874 compared with Grace employee retiring at the same age with the same years of service and salary history.

The GAO concluded as follows: "As currently structured, the Grace retirement program offers potentially greater benefits than the CSRS for most (about two out of three) civil service employees. However, for the civil service employees who retired between the ages of fifty-five and fifty-nine with thirty or more years of service, the CSRS program would provide greater benefits, owing to the reduced annuities for early retirement (retirement before age 62) and less than full cost-of-living adjustments under the Grace pension plan.[15]

Regrettably, grossly exaggerated claims of savings, misrepresentation of facts, and lack of data to support some recommen-

14. Comptroller General, *Comparisons of Retirement Benefits for W. R. Grace and Company and Civil Service Employees,* p. 6.
15. Ibid., p. 10.

dations have created a credibility gap for both poorly and well-supported recommendations of the Grace Commission; and this is a powerful constraint on achieving change. A *Washington Post* editorial of January 15, 1983, said this in part about the Grace Commission report: "If you're inclined to delve into the details of the Report, you should keep three things in mind. The first is that the panel, for all its vaunted private sector efficiency, has produced a report that may set a record for verbosity and impenetrability. . . . A second warning is that most of the savings would come not from eliminating inefficiency, but from cutting services and benefits. . . . A final caution is that none of the Panel's numbers should be taken too seriously."

Legal requirements

Current laws make it harder to achieve change when vested interests are created as a result of benefits bestowed. Furthermore, laws dealing with the civil service usually reflect a balancing of interests; change is harder to achieve when such change would create an unbalanced condition.

When laws were enacted to provide retirement, sick leave, annual leave, and health insurance benefits, they reflected a balancing of costs against the favorable effect on morale, productivity, and recruitment and retention of competent workers. While $32.0 billion of the $49.8 billion in the Grace Commission's estimated savings in personnel management would be secured by reducing health insurance, leave, and retirement benefits, the report sheds little light on the likely impact of such changes on morale, productivity, and recruitment and retention. The GAO has determined that the cutbacks recommended by the Grace Commission are far beyond what might be needed to achieve comparability with the private sector in these benefits.[16] Therefore, it is reasonable to conclude that the recommended reductions, if adopted, not only would lower morale because employees would be convinced that they were being treated unfairly, but also would put the federal government in an unfavorable competitive position for hiring and keeping good workers, and this would have a long-term adverse impact on productivity. These unaddressed negative impacts constitute strong constraints on making the changes proposed by the Grace Commission.

Administrative uncertainty

Frequent turnover of political leadership in the agencies is a primary cause of administrative uncertainty. At the same time

---

16. CBO and GAO, *Analysis of the Grace Commission's Major Proposals,* pp. 252–58.

such turnover often serves as a stimulus for change. However, frequent turnover of political appointees has highlighted the fact that many would-be "change masters" are unsuccessful because they leave as soon as they become sufficiently knowledgeable to serve as effective change agents. They may only be interested in change that will bear fruit during their own short tenure, or their initiative exceeds their capacity. They may have personality characteristics that cause them to turn critics of their policies into hostile personal adversaries. Finally, they might appear so politically partisan that they encourage suspicion about all the changes that they initiate or support.

Many policy changes initiated by an administration that require legislation are not achieved during one Congress. Yet the average time that a presidential appointee remains in government is less than two years. This means that the possibility for change will be enhanced if the permanent leadership (career executives) of the agency recognizes the need. To the degree that career executives are not involved in developing the facts and proposals for change, the likelihood that they will advocate such change is greatly diminished.

Conclusion

The constraints I have discussed can become impenetrable barriers to change, but need they be so? On the one hand, it can be argued that if the Grace Commission had followed a strategy that involved interest groups and congressional committees, the effects would have been deleterious. Such a strategy could have caused delays, diluted recommendations, and greatly reduced claimed savings. Furthermore, a straightforward promotion of factually supported recommendations might have failed to capture the attention of the American people, thereby failing to mobilize the political support necessary for significant change.

On the other hand, it can be argued that the possibilities for achieving change in civil service policies are enhanced by a strategy based on the involvement of interested parties. The parties should be consulted before a particular commission makes recommendations or proposes changes that affect both taxpayers and employees. Both costs and benefits that would flow from adoption of these changes should be analyzed, and the recommendations should be promoted with a scrupulous regard for the facts.

Although the jury is still out on what statutory changes in civil service policies will be achieved with the strategy followed by the Grace Commission, it seems to me that a fundamental question arises. Which of these strategies for achieving change in civil service policies, or perhaps some other strategy, is likely to best serve the public interest, now and in the long term? If, as I believe, the strategy followed by the Grace Commission is not preferable, what should or can be done now, through "late course corrections" to facilitate favorable action on those recommendations of the Grace Commission that are well supported by the facts?

For starters, these late course corrections might be considered. First, put aside the unsupported recommendations, or modify them and the accompanying discussion in accordance with the facts. (The CBO–GAO study identifies most of the problem areas.) Second, inform the president of the changes so that the highest official in our country is not being misled. Third, stop misleading the American people with erroneous oral and written statements about the pay and benefits of federal employees.

Some people may dismiss these proposals as impractical. But remember that reputable corporations recall products that have serious or even minor defects and repair them or replace them with an improved version. The best corporations are also meticulously accurate in the promotion of their products, and even if there were no Federal Trade Commission, those corporations would correct a misleading promotion program.

I believe that taking the actions I have just proposed would clear the poisoned air sufficiently to make possible a new constructive dialogue with the leadership of civil service committees and subcommittees in the House and Senate and the leadership of employee organizations. This would hasten serious consideration of a number of Grace Commission recommendations, many of which have their origins in GAO reports and other studies. For example, basing the pay of clerical, technical, and support jobs on local prevailing rates is not a new idea, nor is changing the current five-step pay range for blue-collar jobs to a three-step structure. Reduced annuities for those retiring at age fifty-five with thirty years of service have also been proposed, as have restraints on cost-of-living adjustments (COLAs) for all entitlement programs including civilian and military retirees and social security recipients. The common feature of all these proposals is the reduction of government expenditures.

However, a constructive dialogue is not likely if the advocates of change insist on discussing each proposal in isolation from other considerations. It would be foolish and probably politically suicidal for the leadership of employee organizations to simply agree that the COLA for retirees should be based on the increase in the CPI or the percentage increase in federal employee pay, whichever is lower. To avoid a "catch 22" situation, such organizations would, as a minimum, probably want simultaneous changes in law to insure that pay adjustments would be authorized in accordance with the Bureau of Labor Statistics surveys of pay in the private sector. This would avoid a repetition of the action taken by the last four presidents to approve adjustments substantially below what the bureau's surveys indicated would achieve comparability. In addition, they would want agreement on criteria that would require the Bureau of Labor Statistics to develop its data by surveying the kind of private sector organizations with which the federal government should compete for professional, scientific, managerial, technical, mechanical, and clerical workers. It is reasonable to assume that the federal government should compete with successful large corporations to recruit and retain the competence required to effectively carry on the operations of government.

Broadening the discussion along these lines will improve the chances for negotiation and consensus. Indeed, a dialogue about comparability based on total compensation, that is, pay, annual leave, sick leave, health care, and retirement benefits, would provide a new opportunity for sensible compromises and agreements. This might be the surest road to significant legislative changes in federal personnel policy.

General Discussion

The discussion began with remarks by Thomas DeYulia, majority staff director of the House Committee on the Post Office and Civil Service. DeYulia said that the Grace Commission has alienated many influential legislators whose assistance is essential for implementing its recommendations. The commission has also antagonized unions and retiree groups, whose support is often necessary before substantive personnel changes can be enacted. If reformers don't have the support of those groups, DeYulia said, at least their neutrality is often necessary. The style and the publicity connected with the commission have raised questions about the Grace Commission's agenda. Is it a political public relations campaign, or does the commission want a serious attempt to analyze difficult public policy issues?

DeYulia said that he strongly disagrees with most of the commission's proposals, but he would like to say a few kind words regarding the commission's strategy. He pointed out that if the primary goal of the Grace Commission is to mobilize public opinion to force changes in public policy, then its strategy makes sense. Since J. Peter Grace has often stated publicly that Congress is part of what he calls the problem, his only avenue was to bypass Congress by means of the mass media and appeal directly to the public to support his proposals. He has done a remarkably good job of that, DeYulia said, but that tactic has made it difficult for Congress to work with the Office of Personnel Management and the executive branch to reach an agreement.

It is too early to tell whether or not Grace's high-risk strategy will work. Like it or not, Grace has seized the political and public relations initiative and provoked a wide-ranging reevaluation by Congress of federal pay and benefits policies.

DeYulia said he doubted whether Grace's proposed reforms will be enacted but Grace has succeeded in at least one respect: there is never any talk of improving federal benefits or federal pay. The talk always focuses on cutting pay and benefits even though almost no improvement in federal fringe benefits has

115

occurred in approximately seven or eight years. DeYulia closed by saying that Grace has succeeded in changing the dialogue, but he has also poisoned the well so that a dispassionate discussion of changes, improvements, and trade-offs in the system's pay and benfits is unlikely.

A. Lee Fritschler asked if the Grace strategy of giving the system a major jolt followed by a public relations campaign isn't the only way to achieve any meaningful change in federal personnel management. He wondered if perhaps people in Washington were overreacting to the commission's strategy.

Rosen responded that he found the commission's strategy distressing because it misled the president. He felt that the letter of transmittal from Grace to the president was very misleading. He said that misleading the president is very serious. In turn the president articulates these misconceptions and reinforces them in the public mind. Rosen added that distorted information excites the public, and the integrity of the government and the confidence of people in government may be damaged in the long run.

Charles Goodsell said that attacks on government are not a way to cure government because they can lead to worse rather than better government. Such attacks promote demoralization, early departures of professionals and experts, and difficulty in recruiting a high caliber of young people into government.

Andrew Feinstein, staff director and chief counsel of the House Subcommittee on Civil Service, said he thought that most of the recommendations will be adopted because of the size of the deficit. He predicted that the deficit will cause a massive congressional reaction next year. Feinstein said he suspected that a substantial portion of the Grace Commission's recommendations will be adopted, whether they are good or bad, justified or unjustified.

DeYulia disagreed with Feinstein by pointing out that the overwhelming number of the Grace Commission's recommendations for change in the personnel management system will not save large amounts of money until twenty years from now, unless retirement benefits are cut substantially for current retirees or pay is cut below its current level.

Patrick Korten said he was glad to see the conversation focusing on a discussion of dollars. He agreed with DeYulia's observation that short-term savings in personnel will not be large enough to significantly shrink the present deficit. However, the most crucial point of the Grace Commission report is that a dollar saved today, assuming no more than about 5 percent inflation a year between now and the year 2000, is twenty-seven dollars saved in the year

2000. The number of dollars saved now, even if relatively small in the short term, will make an enormous difference in the long run.

Korten added that comparability between the federal retirement system and practices in the private sector is the greatest area of disagreement in discussions of the Grace Commission's personnel recommendations. He pointed out that the most serious difference between the two systems is the virtual absence in the private sector of automatic full indexation of the cost of living. He said that the real public policy question is, should federal civil servants be receiving a retirement benefit that is radically different from what is available in the private sector?

DeYulia responded that Korten had overlooked the items in the private sector retirement practices that are more generous than those in the federal system such as capital accumulation plans; coordination with social security, which is 100 percent fully indexed; and the federal requirement of thirty years of service. DeYulia said that the OPM emphasizes the areas of federal benefits that are most attractive and ignores the less attractive aspects of the total compensation package. He observed that a yardstick is needed for the comparison of total compensation in the federal sector with that in the private sector.

Korten asked DeYulia if he would be willing to accept adjustments in other areas of compensation to make them more comparable with practices in the private sector. Korten asked DeYulia if at the same time, he would accept unreduced retirement benefits no earlier than age sixty-two, which is what the commission recommends (OPM recommends age sixty-five). And, Korten asked if DeYulia would favor, for example, taking the social security maximum and agreeing to fully index that amount for federal retirees, with either no index or a restricted index for the balance.

DeYulia responded that his committee has always been willing to discuss and evaluate OPM proposals. He asked Korten if the OPM would allow pay comparability based on the Professional, Administrative, and Technical Survey to go into effect instead of always sending up an alternative pay plan because in the OPM's view the Professional, Administrative, and Technical Survey is flawed.

Korten responded yes, once a survey is used that includes 100 percent of the firms in the market as its sample.

Comarow said that he thought that the commission had made a tactical mistake by not consulting with Congress and the unions.

Even if the chances are great that the commission wouldn't agree with them, there was a slight chance the commission might have picked up a good idea or two; learned what the counterarguments are; and deprived its opponents of complaining that they were never consulted. The key point, Comarow said, is that the political choice is not between consultation and public support. First, seek participation through consultation, and then try to gain public support.

James Lawler said that much of the criticism of the Grace Commission's work is unfair. Given the constraints facing the commission, the quality of the work is variable but generally high, and the savings claimed are probably low. He felt that the criticisms of the commission's work are unjustified, especially the claim that Grace is bypassing the normal decisionmaking process because he is going directly to the American people. Furthermore, the statement that the savings proposed by the Grace Commission are relatively small is contradicted by the long-term savings of, for example, $58 billion twenty years from now if the military and civilian retirement plans are changed.

John Post, resident consultant at Brookings, said that a number of the criticisms of the commission's report in terms of methodology are well founded. He felt that many of the chief executives who signed the report have not participated in the discussion about the report. Post added that the driving force behind reform should be not only the deficit but also a desire to design a better compensation system.

Post said that the atmosphere surrounding the Grace Commission is so controversial that a better way to proceed is to break up the report into its separate parts. People who were responsible for those parts of the report should promote them.

Feinstein said that the presidential role is more essential than the commission's role in promoting a package of substantial budget cuts. Budget cuts must be viewed as affecting all people equally. The Grace Commission's recommendations, or at least some of them, will clearly be part of such a package.

Levine concluded the conference by noting that the massive federal deficit is likely to force many of the Grace Commission's ideas before Congress in 1985 as part of a deficit reduction package. In federal personnel management, the critical issue is how to build a better yet less costly system in the public interest.

O. Glenn Stahl summarized the conference by identifying the controversial subjects discussed as well as subjects on which a considerable amount of consensus occurred. Stahl suggested that a similar conference be held just to tackle the issues raised by the federal retirement system. Such a conference would cover private sector practices and their comparability with federal practices, particularly in retirement eligibility and benefits. Stahl noted the serious inadequacy of the information about the federal service and the problem of too little consciousness of managerial responsibilities by key federal workers, particularly political appointees. The selection and training of these people remain matters of concern. Another important issue is whether dollars or public purposes provide the best criteria for evaluating the public service. The appropriateness and the effects of the derogation of the bureaucracy and bureaucrats also seem to be serious concerns.

Stahl said that the unique occupational profile of the federal service with its heavy concentration of professionals and technical employees, unlike almost all of the private sector, has obvious and continuing effects on pay, benefits, and the so-called bulge in the middle grades. Employee motivation is also important to the federal system. How can employee motivation be improved? How far can delegation go in the public service? Clearly, private sector models and profit and loss controls do not apply. Should the models instead be based on experience in other nations or in state and local governments? Conference participants agreed about the need for more research and demonstration projects. A good deal of discussion also occurred about the political climate of public service and how it affects expectations of good performance among the middle and upper levels of management.

Whether to establish an independent Office of Federal Management is a question that deserves investigation. The progress made by individual agencies in improving personnel management and productivity needs to be better monitored and shared throughout the rest of the government. The role of professional managers, scientists, and technical employees in the Senior Executive Service should be examined, along with a renewed concern for their education and training. Stahl observed that the constraints on personnel reform are difficult but penetrable, especially if more time and effort are spent on reform. Finally, how should study commissions like the President's Private Sector Survey on Cost Control proceed, especially in regard to consulting with Congress and interest groups? Generally speaking, he felt that consultation and broad participation enhance the chances of winning acceptance and implementation.

As the conference closed, participants agreed that some changes in the federal personnel system are inevitable, that more discussion of specific issues will be helpful, and that the key participants in Congress and the administration must find new ways of reaching compromises before a better system can be designed and implemented.

Appendix: A Summary of the Personnel Report of the Grace Commission

Civil Service Retirement System

Are retirement benefits overly liberal, acting as an incentive to early retirement?

Findings. "There is an imbalance between consideration of Government and taxpayer interests and employee wishes in the matter of early retirement, in favor of the employee" (p. 32). The task force found that "there is no stated CSRS [civil service retirement system] objective" (p. 12). It therefore established its objective as threefold: to provide financial security competitive with major private sector plans (which include social security) while not incurring excessive costs; to open opportunities for promotable younger employees; and to provide benefit incentives that attract and retain competent personnel.

The task force found the civil service retirement system "significantly more costly than the average private sector pension program" (p. 11). The federal government pays the equivalent of 29 percent of its payroll in pension benefits, compared with only 14 percent in the private sector. This comparison understates the problem because of the large portion of unfunded federal pension liability, which if included (amortized over forty years) would bring the federal figure to 85 percent of payroll.

Federal employees retire earlier, on average, than private sector employees; they "obtain greater benefits under normal and disability retirement" and are protected by cost-of-living adjustments in benefits "far" in excess of retirees in the private sector (p. 13).

The task force believes that its recommendations, in addition to meeting the three stated objectives of the civil service retirement

Note: Janet Garry summarized the information for this appendix. Page references throughout are to the President's Private Sector Survey on Cost Control (the Grace Commission), *Report on Personnel Management* (Washington, D.C.: PPSSCC, 1983).

* Throughout this appendix asterisks indicate the necessity of congressional modification of existing law or introduction of new legislation to implement the task force's recommendation.

121

system, address problems of appropriate rewards for employee contributions (service and salary); employee reception; adaptability to legislative, regulatory, and economic environments; facility of administration; avoidance of excessive early retirement; absence of federal long-term disability plan; and "inequities in CSRS which favor some annuitants over others" (p. 18).

The task force also said that federal employees "aggressively pursue early retirement" (p. 26). The extra years employees spend on retirement are not offset entirely by the savings over paying an increased annuity for longer service. In addition, there is the government's loss of employee knowledge, skill, and experience.

Recommendations. Numbers 1-1 through 1-8, pp. 29–53, include the following:

—Raise normal retirement age for unreduced pension to age sixty-two (from fifty-five) applicable to all new employees and all current employees under age forty-five. The full retirement benefits currently allowed—at age fifty-five after thirty years' service, at age sixty after twenty years' service—occur in only 4 percent to 6 percent of private sector firms. Under social security, full retirement is not available until after age sixty-five.*

—Base CSRS benefits on average employee salary over five years instead of three, which will bring the federal government practice in line with over 80 percent of the private sector plans as reported by Bankers Trust and Hay.*

—Discontinue crediting unused sick leave as extra service under the CSRS: "We know of no instance in the private sector where the practice is to count unused sick leave as service under the retirement plan."*

—Reduce partial pension benefits at twice the current rate— one-third percent rather than one-sixth percent—for each month retirement precedes age sixty-two; penalize agencies that use early retirement provisions "to solve staffing problems."*

—Remove the disability provision from the CSRS. It currently underpays (compared with the private sector) short-term employees and employees with families while permitting payments to some individuals still capable of working. Establish a separate long-term disability plan adhering to private sector practices.*

—Change death benefits to take account of actual ages of retirees and spouses to correct for current CSRS inequity, which benefits married annuitants and is disadvantageous to single retirees. Eliminate benefits providing payments to assist surviving children with postsecondary educations; there is "no counterpart in the private sector."*

—Change overly liberal cost-of-living adjustments (COLAs). Base them on the Consumer Price Index or general schedule pay increases, whichever is lower, in order to eliminate increases for retirees that are greater than wage increases for active employees. Limit COLAs for retirees whose annuities exceed those payable to current retirees (due to overindexing from 1969 to 1976). Bring future COLAs in line with private sector practices: automatic COLAs such as the federal government's occur in less than 10 percent of private sector plans.*

—Federal employees should be covered under social security, on the following basis: mandatory for new employees and all current employees under age forty-five; optional coverage on a one-time election basis for employees age forty-five and over; integrate the CSRS with social security on a basis comparable to private sector prevailing practice; revise the CSRS for those employees not covered by social security to "correct serious divergences from private practices (pensions plus social security) and to remove windfall benefits."*

Federal Employees Health Benefit Program

Can the federal employees health benefit program (FEHBP) be made more cost effective while still maintaining adequate coverage?

Findings. "The total cost of FEHBP exceeded private sector, non-manufacturing experience by 1 percent of the payroll, or $618 million in 1981" (p. 56), and "the average total 1981 health benefit cost per Federal employee was higher than comparable private sector cost by as much as 40 percent" (p. 60).

The task force "assumed that the objective of the FEHBP was to provide a measure of assistance to Federal employees in financing their hospital and other medical expenses" (p. 58). The federal employees health benefit program covers 73 percent of claims, compared with 82 percent in the private sector, due to the program's greater participant cost-sharing features. But, the program has no maximum benefit, as many private sector plans do, and the program coordinates its benefits with medicare to eliminate coverage gaps, whereas private sector plans subtract medicare benefits with no fill-in.

The federal government's annual share of health benefit costs, currently 24 percent, is increasing faster than the private sector firms' share, now only 17 percent. The federal employees health benefit program's contribution formula causes government's share to rise automatically when premiums rise, and the government's percentage contribution varies widely with the plan selected by the employee. The choice of many plans, frequency of choice changes, and variation in benefits and premiums facilitate movement to plans with high coverage by employees who expect expensive medical costs and also lead to high administration costs. Private sector counterparts have little or no choice. There is a large and growing proportion of retirees and disability annuitants as participants in the health benefit program (from 10 percent in 1969 to 36.6 percent in 1981).[1]

Recommendations. Numbers 2-1 through 2-16, pp. 61–63, include the following:

—Open enrollment every other year rather than yearly.

—Limit choice of health maintenance organizations within geographic areas.

—Develop bid-obtaining program to encourage vendor participation.

—Improve information flow.

—Eliminate 75 percent government contribution ceiling.* This proposal assumes that employees will choose a lower premium plan if government pays a larger contribution.

—Vary premiums by geographic area.

—Require that benefits for annuitants be included as part of their agencies' budgets "to focus attention on the high costs of those benefits."*

—Bring the annuitant and survivor eligibility requirements in line with the private sector's and authorize establishment of a project to explore procompetition approaches, such as the voucher (fixed amount) payment system.*

Annual Leave

Can costs of vacation time be reduced by amending the annual leave policy to conform with private sector practices?

Findings. The federal government's practice of giving vacation after only three months' service compares with less than 24 percent of private sector firms included in the survey.

The federal government provides more liberal accrual of leave time, most notable in the three to five years of service category, where the federal worker receives twenty days annually and the private sector worker receives only ten days annually.

In 52 percent of private sector firms, all unused vacation is

1. For its analysis, the task force used the *Review of the Federal Employees Health Benefits Program* (William H. Mercer, 1982); the U.S. Chamber of Commerce report "Employee Benefits, 1980"; and Hay Associates, *1981 Noncash Compensation Comparison.*

forfeited, whereas federal employees only forfeit any excess over thirty days.

Recommendations. Those on pp. 68–69 include the following:

—Require six months of continual service for vacation eligibility.*

—Adjust annual accrual rate downward (three to five years' service receives twelve days, with more gradual increases to the maximum of twenty-six days at twenty-five years rather than fifteen years).*

—Change policy to forfeiture of unused leave from effective date of change.*

Sick Leave

Can sick leave costs be reduced by bringing leave policy into closer conformance with private sector practices?

Findings. The federal government allows thirteen days annual paid sick leave. Employees, on average, use nine and accumulate four. The task force finds usage excessive compared with the nonmanufacturing private sector, where 5.5 days is the average annual sick leave usage.

The task force finds federal sickness and accident disability protection more expensive, more liberal in maximum accumulation of sick leave days and exchange of sick leave for credited service, but less comprehensive "with respect to the gap between sick leave and CSRS" (p. 76).

Recommendations. Those on pp. 76–78 include the following:

—Set maximum carry-forward accumulation of 130 days sick leave.*

—Eliminate the crediting of unused sick leave as service time in computing annuities.*

—Sick leave recommendations are coordinated with and assume implementation of the CSRS recommendations. The task force believes that once CSRS is amended to require that an employee be sixty-five to be eligible for disability retirement, employees can be persuaded of the importance of accumulating the full 130 days of sick leave "to bridge the gap between the date of disability and the commencement of long-term disability benefits."

Compensation and classification system

Federal Position Classification System

Can excessive costs due to overgrading and administration be reduced? Can individual agencies be held more accountable for position management?

Findings. Currently all federal government white-collar occupations are grouped under eighteen general schedule grades. Position overgrading is high.

Classification gamesmanship is informally accepted, and managers receive no reward for proper classification or position management. Rather than appropriately using "special rates" available for recruiting purposes, overrating is used both to attract qualified applicants and to increase pay, stepping up the eighteen-year span intended for moving through the grades. Seventy-two percent of "exempt" federal employees are rated GS–11 or higher; comparable positions in the private sector are held by only 26 percent of the white-collar work force.

The classification system is perceived by managers as inflexible and slow, blocking their ability to "promptly assess and effectively react to changing or unusual problems" (p. 88). The formal standards for position ranking vary in length and include superfluous information, whereas private sector samples were "uniformly shorter and much easier to understand" (p. 84). Many standards are outdated: half exceed ten years in age. The Office of Personnel Management and the Office of Management and Budget both assert that primary responsibility for corrective action belongs to the other.

When within-grade step increases, quality step increases, and promotion increases are considered in addition to the automatic annual comparability increase, earnings growth in federal service is much higher than publicized.

In the private sector, responsibility for classification and pay is under one authority. The Office of Personnel Management suffers "fragmentation" (p. 90) as responsibility is shared by three associate directors.

Recommendations. Numbers 5-1 through 5-8, pp. 94–96, include the following:

—Redesign and simplify the classification standards format.

—Reduce overgrading by establishing a single authority with management objectives; issue position papers to agencies for performance appraisal; require the use of special rates, incentive awards, and quality step increases rather than overgrading; require that agencies submit quarterly position management reports to the Office of Personnel Management and the Office of Management and Budget; protect classifiers from pressure to misgrade.

—Through presidential direction, phase out overgrading of positions.

—Through presidential memo, give the Office of Personnel

Management primary authority to direct agencies; evaluate agency implementation efforts.

—Make sure that the Office of Personnel Management and the Office of Management and Budget cooperate in crediting performing agencies via their "budget dealings with OMB."

Pay Comparability (white collar)

Is pay comparability as currently structured a sound approach for the federal sector?

Findings. Pay comparability is based on the National Survey of Professional, Administrative, Technical, and Clerical Pay (PATC survey) done annually by the Department of Labor. The greatest problem with this survey is that it is narrow in scope. For instance, less than 25 percent of federal positions are covered (only 1.7 percent of federal administrative positions, compared with 27 percent of the federal work force actually in administrative positions). The survey covers only ninety-six work levels of twenty-four occupational categories (yet there are 425 different federal occupations). The survey uses a private sector sample that is nonrepresentative, skewed toward highly skilled jobs and highly paid jobs that set salaries for GS–12 through GS–15. Overall, only 25 percent of employees in the private white-collar work force are represented. Furthermore, small- and medium-sized firms (with fewer than fifty people) are not surveyed, which eliminates over 95 percent of firms in all major sectors. Finally, state and local government and nonprofit organizations are excluded. Although workers in these areas were previously small in number, now an estimated 30 percent of the white-collar work force is represented here.

In addition, there are problems with the inflexibility of the general schedule system itself. Pay scales are not localized, as they are in the private sector, and "use of the General Schedule nationwide for all Federal jobs has created and perpetuates gross pay inequities. For an entity as large, diverse, and complex as the Federal Government, it is unrealistic to believe that all of the approximately 425 different occupations can be slotted into 15 pay grades" (p. 105).

Recommendations. Numbers 6-1 through 6-6, pp. 105–106, include the following:

—Expand the PATC survey to include a greater number of jobs: the "full spectrum of positions at all levels."

—Conduct the survey every other year, using interim estimates.*

—Include state and local government and nonprofit organizations in the PATC survey.*

—Include firms in the PATC survey with as few as twenty-five employees.

—Set clerical, technical, and support salaries according to locally prevailing rates.*

—Expand the general schedule to more than fifteen basic pay levels.*

Pay Comparability (blue collar)

Is the federal wage system (FWS) designed and administered so that pay comparability is achieved as intended?

Findings. The "present pay plan design and administration does not result in true pay comparability" (p. 108). Pay levels are significantly above local private sector rates. The Office of Personnel Management prescribes practices and procedures of implementing and administering the federal wage system in consultation with labor organizations. Each executive agency head is responsible, within the guidelines set by the Office of Personnel Management, for fixing and administering rates of pay. Problems with using the prevailing rate include the current use of a five-step rate structure with pay comparability entering at step two while the average pay position is step four (108 percent of step two) and delocalization of pay comparability due to the Monroney Amendment, "which provides that under certain conditions Federal rates can be set from wage data procured from outside the local rates area" (p. 108). There are also nationwide night shift differentials not consistent with the private sector in many geographic areas and "perceived" overtime inequities due to dual calculations, under both the U.S. Code and the Fair Labor Standards Act.

Recommendations. Numbers 7-1 through 7-5, p. 111, include the following:

—Redesign the five-step pay range to three steps, with step two at 100 percent of the prevailing rate and a ceiling of 105 percent at step three.*

—Include state and local government and nonprofit organizations in rate setting.*

—Repeal the Monroney Amendment.*

—Repeal nationwide night shift differentials and set differentials on a local basis.*

—Provide a single method of computation of overtime.*

Executive Level and Senior Executive Service Pay

Is the current method of setting pay for the executive levels and the Senior Executive Service appropriate?

Findings. The following quotation is from Charles Bowsher, the comptroller general, November 1981. "Since March 1977 (four years) the executive pay ceiling has been increased by only 5.5 percent. During that same period, retired federal executives received annuity cost-of-living adjustments totaling 55 percent; federal white-collar pay rates have been increased by 38 percent and private sector executive pay has gone up about 40 percent (p. 112)."

Major problems revealed by the task force include linkage of SES and GS–16 through GS–18 salaries to the executive schedule levels IV and V. By law, no member of the Senior Executive Service can receive a salary higher than the pay rate for level IV of the executive schedule; and no GS–16 through GS–18 employee can be paid a salary greater than that of level V of the executive schedule. This restriction leads to pay compression, in which people at different levels of position are being paid the same salary. Salaries are unrealistically low and unfair at some levels. Furthermore, retirement is becoming more financially rewarding than working for many federal executives. Between 1977 and 1981, the average length of executive experience dropped nearly 50 percent.

Pay compression leads to low morale and decreased productivity. Too little financial reward exists even for GS–15s to join the Senior Executive Service because compression extends downward to the GS–15 level. This group is also retiring early. The bonus program of the Senior Executive Service suffers a lack of credibility. Employees believe that bonuses depend on the visibility and priority of projects rather than performance excellence.

Finally, employees believe that the Senior Executive Service is too large. Overinclusiveness has driven membership to 6,800. Some observers suggest that it be reduced to half that size or less.

Recommendations. Numbers 8-1 and 8-2, p. 119, include the following:

—The Office of Personnel Management should investigate which positions in the Senior Executive Service have the scope, accountability, and impact to warrant bonus eligibility and a higher salary schedule and should eliminate staff support functions as executive level positions. There should be no pay linkage between proposed new increases in the Senior Executive Service and the executive schedule.

—Develop legislation to increase executive level and salary ranges in the Senior Executive Service by 20 percent to 30 percent; provide 10 percent to 15 percent salary differential between each of the executive levels; provide annual or biannual review of executive schedule salaries; separate the salary of members of Congress from the executive schedule.*

Personnel management operations

The Employment Process and Public Information

Can the Office of Personnel Management modify the process of providing public information regarding job openings in order to reduce the number of inquiries to those applicants reasonably suitable and qualified for available positions? Will restricting the number of applicant inquiries adversely affect the quality of applicants for certification?

Findings. The staffing group of the Office of Personnel Management works closely with the agencies in developing examining procedures, recruiting, evaluating applicants, and creating classification and qualification standards. They also assist agencies in preparing internal merit promotion programs.

Public information is disseminated by the Office of Personnel Management through ten regional and forty-four area offices. Under the area offices are sixty-one job information centers that also provide centralized testing; forty-eight of these provide computer services.

Despite cutbacks in the program (largely cutbacks in hours of area office operations), in 1982 there were still more than seventy inquiries for each position filled. "OPM officials expressed concern that the cost of responding to applicant inquiries is too high when compared to the number of individuals who ultimately obtain jobs" (p. 125).

There is a need for uniform methods of targeting applicants geographically as well as occupationally. Practical targeting requires a cooperative effort of the Office of Personnel Management and the hiring agency. Of noteworthy success are instances where a hiring agency's initiative and expenditure have been used to supplement the public notice support provided by the Office of Personnel Management.

In addition to each agency's efforts, public efforts and responsibility are sought: "OPM recognizes the statutory obligation to provide timely public information. However, because of conditions dictated by the current economic environment, the public should assume a portion of the responsibility to seek out opportunities available with the Government." (p. 126).

Recommendations. Numbers 9-1 through 9-3, pp. 126, 127, include the following:

—The staffing group of the Office of Personnel Management should reevaluate and define goals in information provision, setting guidelines to limit applicant inquiries to "ensure optimum return on the public information investment."

—The Office of Personnel Management should "direct only those communications with the greatest potential for meeting the needs of both the agency and the general public. Higher quality intake should be reflected by higher scores in the applicant rankings."

—The Office of Personnel Management should increase the development of automation techniques to respond to inquiries in a faster, more complete, and cost-effective way.

The Employment Process and Automated Examining

Should the Office of Personnel Management assign priority to the control and development of "distributed automated examining systems"?

Findings. Due to cutbacks since the late 1970s, the average ratio of federal personnel serviced to staffing personnel within the office's ten regions is approximately 1,100 to 1, extremely high when compared with that of the private sector. Experienced staffing personnel are leaving. Budget cuts and staff decreases lengthen processing time for agency requests. In 1982 the examining process (administration and evaluation of written tests and applications, referral to agencies) required 57 percent of the staffing group's labor hours and 47 percent of the staffing group's budget.

Other problems identified by the task force include the time-consuming, subjective ranking of narrative responses on application forms. There is currently a scarcity of trained staff to process these applications. And currently, only those offices with automated examining procedures are "able to cope" (p. 131) with the work load. "If the levels of agency staffing activity increase even moderately during FY 1983, the Staffing Group will be unable to respond with quality examining service at present staff levels. Only those area offices having automated examining systems will be able to handle agency workloads in a responsive and professional manner" (p. 134). The alternative is that the hiring agencies will have to take over more of the work load from the Office of Personnel Management.

Since 1978 the staffing group has developed a "distributive system" of minicomputers in all regions, utilizing the Macon Service Center for test scoring and processing. This system has proven more time and cost effective than traditional manual processing. Development efforts were slow because of incompatible mainframes, control of the mainframe outside the staffing group, and the lack of priorities set by the Office of Personnel Management for system design. The Office of Personnel Management failed to recognize the impact and potential of automated examining.

Recommendation. The recommendation on p. 135 is as follows:

—The Office of Personnel Management should establish as high priority the substantial expansion of automated examining programs.

Reductions in Force

Could changes or modifications to the current reduction-in-force procedures reduce disruption, lower costs, and preserve quality in the work force without adversely affecting employee rights?

Findings. The Office of Personnel Management prescribes regulations for releasing employees during action to reduce the size of the work force. "These regulations must be followed by Federal agencies separating employees because of shortage of funds, lack of work, reorganization, reclassification due to change of duties, or the need to place a person returning with reemployment rights" (p. 137).

There are negative effects of the current system. Areas of agency concern over procedures for reductions in force include competitive levels, tenure groups, bump and retreat rights, and the weight of performance appraisals.

The task force also found that performance and efficiency play a small part in determining actions during a reduction in force. Bump and retreat rights result in indiscriminant displacement and loss of valued employees. Veterans' preference has excessive weight. Grade and pay retention for two years following demotion adversely affects the savings benefit of conducting a reduction in force. Finally, relocation, retraining, and lowered morale are substantial costs to agencies of reductions in force.

Recommendations. Numbers 11-1 through 11-8, pp. 143–146, include the following:

—Alter the competitive area for employee relocation (currently defined as geographical area and bureaucratic unit) to "non-clerical" or "clerical within geographic commuting areas but across bureaucratic units." This will lessen the disruption caused by displacement of "highly skilled clerical employees by marginally skilled or unskilled nonclerical employees."

—Establish separate competitive levels for specific occupational levels to include only positions similar in qualifications, duties, and responsibilities.

—Put "preference eligibility" and outstanding performance on an equal basis by ranking employees with points for length of service, performance, and preference eligibility.

—Limit bump and retreat rights to one grade level lower than the old position.

—Limit reemployment listing to one year; require periodic interest indicators from separated employees; require agencies to make offers to any fully qualified employee; remove employee from the list once a comparable position is declined.

Permanent Employment versus Contracted Services

Can federal functions that are "basically commerical in nature" (p. 151) be contracted out to the private sector at a lesser cost?

Findings. The Office of Management and Budget establishes and oversees policies and regulations for federal procurement. For an agency to contract out, the office requires savings of 10 percent in related personnel costs; a contractor to hire displaced government employees; and proof of efficient agency operations prior to comparative studies.

Despite endorsement of cost-saving contracting, a 1978 survey report from the General Accounting Office stated that Circular A-76, the major tool for implementing contracting procedures, was not perceived by managers as fully supported national policy. Some agencies cite the following as reasons they do not contract out: fear of loss of control, complex and time-consuming cost comparison procedures, fear of private business failures, and union problems.

Recommendation. The recommendation on p. 155 is as follows:

—The Office of Management and Budget should prepare legislation that mandates agencies to conduct and implement the results of cost comparison analyses on all functional areas as outlined by OMB Circular A-76. Legislation should be passed that would establish a national policy on acquiring goods and services from the private sector when justified on the basis of cost; provide the Office of Management and Budget with authority to approve exemptions to the general policy; and provide for a less complex system of cost comparison.*

Training and development services

Instructional Television Production Facilities

Should the Office of Personnel Management act as "broker" to coordinate utilization of the approximately twenty-five separate government-operated television studios in the Washington, D.C.–Baltimore area?

Findings. A survey of members of the Office of Personnel Management's instructional systems development branch and TV specialists from the resource sharing group revealed that 67 percent of employees favored centralized coordination effort; a clearinghouse approach was suggested.

The task force also found a current 33 percent underutilization rate and some agencies contracting out. An analysis of eighteen fully in-house productions that used resource sharing evidenced substantial cuts in production costs. Expensive idle time is a function of underutilization, both of sophisticated electronic equipment and of highly salaried technical staff.

Recommendations. Numbers 13-1 through 13-3, pp. 159–160, include the following:

—The Office of Personnel Management, acting as a broker, should match user agencies with studios most capable of delivering needed products and services.

—The Office of Personnel Management, the Office of Management and Budget, and the General Services Administration should develop together a simplified procurement system to expedite and centralize agencies' out-of-house requirements.

—The Office of Personnel Management should establish a simplified accounting system to accommodate interagency and in-house–outside contractor fund transfers.

Implementation of the recommendations will be enhanced by a marketing effort to promote these activities.

Duplication of Supervisory Training

Could more centrally controlled and guided management training programs under the Office of Personnel Management result in better quality and lower cost of such programs?

Findings. Although the Office of Personnel Management is not specifically authorized to prescribe or regulate the details of intraagency training programs, it authorizes "the issuance of regulations containing the standards and principles under which intraagency training programs are to operate" (p. 162).

A more systematic approach to the training and development effort could result in improved morale, improved management, improved executive performance and overall organization effectiveness, in addition to cost savings.

Sufficient evidence exists, based on interviews with central agency training officers and print-outs of contract actions (all procurement actions for training contracts exceeding $10,000 in fiscal 1981 were randomly sampled) "to conclude that no standard practice exists for the contracting of generic training program offerings" (p. 168).

The Office of Personnel Management is not sought as a first choice for filling an agency's supervisory training needs. Attempts to prevent duplicating efforts are sometimes intentionally avoided: some agencies "customize" (p. 168) to avoid using the Office of Personnel Management courses and curriculum materials, even when programs are similar in content and approach. Finally, agencies are under little auditing control for their expenditures of funds for discretionary generic training.

Recommendations. Numbers 14-1 through 14-6, pp. 168–169, include the following:

—The Office of Personnel Management should determine what generic training programs will meet the basic needs of agencies by identifying skills and competencies required throughout the federal government.

—The office should design mechanisms by which these skills can be mastered.

—The office should develop a "train the trainer" program to certify agency personnel conducting supervisory training.

—The office should institute auditing and tracking procedures.

—The Office of Personnel Management and the Office of Management and Budget should monitor agency proposals in order to identify duplication.

Implementation, if resisted, may require "Executive Order authority to bring about the desired results" (p. 170).

Executive Seminar Center Operations

Can current operating costs of the Office of Personnel Management's executive seminar centers be reduced through improved productivity and more efficient facilities utilization?

Findings. The executive seminar center operations fall under the jurisdiction of the executive and management development branch of the work force effectiveness and development group. The executive seminar centers are residential interagency training and development facilities that aid agencies in meeting programmatic, executive, and managerial needs.

The Kings Point, New York, center serves the east coast, or over 113,000 GS–13 to GS–15 employees. At a ceiling of thirty-eight students per session, it is too small to accommodate the area it serves. Although the Merchant Marine Academy location keeps current operating costs low, the small capacity, marginal housing, and problems of food service suggest relocation of this center. The Oak Ridge, Tennessee, center serves over 47,000 employees in the middle states. With a capacity of seventy students, it was underutilized in 1982. The Denver, Colorado, center is poorly geographically situated in relation to the far west. The Pacific Coast GS–13 to GS–15 employee population of over 21,000 is nearly double the corresponding population in the mountain states. Agency travel costs from the western region are high.

Each resident staff consists of professional, educational, and developmental specialists, supplemented by visiting faculty drawn from leadership in government, business, industry, and academia. Staff (four or five per center and one director) are underutilized at all locations. Active seminar time for each is from sixteen to twenty weeks annually.

Recommendations. Numbers 15-1 through 15-5, p. 177, include the following:

—The Office of Personnel Management should initiate a site search in California and in the Washington, D.C.–New England corridor, completing a cost comparison of potential sites to determine final locations responsive to the demographics of the population distribution.

—The office should monitor use of the Oak Ridge center and relinquish excess, non-cost-effective space.

—Professional staff at each center should be cut to three, with active time increased to twenty-eight weeks annually for each staff member.

Organization planning and productivity

Productivity

Should the federal government establish a central office with the responsibility to promote and coordinate formal, visible programs for productivity improvements throughout its operations?

Findings. Over the past few years, leadership responsibility for federal productivity improvement efforts has been shifted among the Office of Management and Budget, the joint financial management improvement program, the National Center for Productivity and Quality of Working Life, and the Office of Personnel Management. Although support exists for productivity improvement at all levels in federal management, "very little visibility and priority is provided for an organized formal approach" (p. 182).

In cases where productivity programs are formalized, successful results are evident. For instance, the National Labor Relations Board instituted, twenty years ago, a case management system that increases productivity between 2 percent and 12 percent each year, and the Department of Agriculture's National Finance Office, through centralization and automation, has reduced the cost of processing voucher payments from $12.00 to $2.50 per voucher.

A 1980 report by the General Accounting Office, *Improving the Productivity of Federal Payment Centers Could Save Millions,* states, "Productivity should be a prime concern of Government managers at all levels. . . . Government payment centers could save millions in labor costs by developing measures of productivity and implementing identified improvement techniques" (p. 182).

Recommendations. Numbers 16-1 through 16-5, p. 182, include the following:

—The Office of Management and Budget should be directed to establish a permanent office to develop, promote, and coordinate governmentwide programs to improve productivity. Staff and resource support should be provided by the Office of Personnel Management.

—The Office of Management and Budget and the Office of Personnel Management should utilize existing incentive awards (for example, the president's award for distinguished federal service, presidential management improvement awards, and the employee suggestion program) to recognize managers whose contributions improve productivity.

—Performance evaluations should reflect productivity effort participation for both managers and subordinates.

—The Office of Management and Budget should identify and eliminate all disincentives to productivity improvement.

Duplication of Personnel Services

Can federal agencies consolidate certain personnel offices and services?

Findings. Over 1,700 separate personnel offices in Washington, D.C., and in the field employ 45,000 people to plan and execute personnel policies and procedures for various federal agencies within guidelines set by the Office of Personnel Management. Decentralization occurs within agencies and departments as field offices and installations address the specific personnel requirements of their agencies and departments.

Several models for organizing field personnel already exist. For instance, the Department of Defense has made an effort to consolidate personnel servicing offices for the armed forces and the Defense Logistics Agency, primarily for training, recruitment, and information services. The Department of Labor consolidates personnel offices, and the Department of Health and Human Services consolidates offices and services under the assistant secretary for personnel; twenty-six regional offices have been merged into ten branches. The Department of Agriculture's food safety and inspection service (FSIS) "has the only truly centralized personnel servicing system discovered in the course of this review (p. 188)" with only one personnel servicing office for the country, located in Minneapolis. This office handles all personnel activities other than labor relations; no personnel specialists are required at individual FSIS locations because clerks provide Minneapolis with all necessary information.

There are major problems with centralization in the federal government. For example, the highly decentralized nature of the government has allowed a great deal of autonomy for agencies and bureaus within them, which interferes with consolidation for bureaucratic reasons. Furthermore, consolidation of personnel services may be counter to the practice of delegating management authority to the lowest practical level of accountability, which requires that management support functions remain close to the location of the manager.

Recommendations. Numbers 17-1 through 17-5, pp. 191–192, include the following:

—Department and agency heads should direct line managers to report on possibilities for the consolidation of field office personnel functions; departments and agencies should forward a summary of the results to the Office of Personnel Management and the Office of Management and Budget.

—Agency heads should share personnel administrative services.

—Agencies should establish a minimum number of staff and a minimum supervisor grade level for field personnel offices.

—The Office of Personnel Management should encourage

smaller agencies to obtain their personnel services from either the General Services Administration or a department with a large personnel operation.

Work Force Planning

Should the federal government have a uniform work force planning method for use within the agencies?

Findings. Although there is no commonly accepted definition of work force planning, it can be described as the performance of those planning tasks to determine (1) the staffing requirements of an organization and (2) the management work load to obtain, develop, and maintain the needed work force.

No standards currently guide the agencies on work force planning, although some agencies have developed internal planning processes.

The Office of Personnel Management and the agencies give a low priority to work force planning. "The limited capacity of the agencies to provide reliable information to the Administration and Congress on their workforce needs tends to limit sound decision making on human resource programs and policies" (p. 195).

There is a consensus among management representatives of the General Accounting Office, the Department of the Army, the Department of the Navy, the Internal Revenue Service, the Office of Personnel Management, and the Office of Management and Budget in favor of a "common workforce planning program" for use in all agencies. However, skepticism about implementation is based on budget uncertainties, cutbacks, reductions in force, and changes in the political environment. The task force believes these problems are overemphasized.

Recommendations. Numbers 18-1 through 18-4, p. 197, include the following:

—The Office of Personnel Management, with the assistance of the private sector professionals serving as consultants, should develop a work force planning policy and a framework of procedures for use by the agencies.

—After a one-year testing period at two agencies, monitored by the Office of Management and Budget, if the project is successful, the Office of Personnel Management should require its adoption by all federal agencies.

Conference Participants

Sheb Adkisson
Staff Assistant, Senate Subcommittee on Civil Service, Post Office, and General Services

Earl A. Armbrust
Deputy Assistant Director for General Government, Congressional Budget Office

Duncan Bailey
Associate Professor of Economics, University of South Carolina

J. P. Bolduc
Senior Vice-President, W. R. Grace & Co., and Chief Operating Officer, President's Private Sector Survey on Cost Control

Bun B. Bray, Jr.
Executive Director, Federal Managers Association

Judith Cahill
Vice-President, Hay/Huggins Company, Inc.

Colin Campbell, S.J.
Professor, Georgetown University

William G. Colman
Director of Research, National Committee on Public Employee Pensions

Murray Comarow
Distinguished Adjunct Professor in Residence, The American University

James S. Cowan
Special Counsel, Senate Subcommittee on Civil Service, Post Office, and General Services

J. Craig Cumbey
Deputy Assistant Secretary of the Air Force, Civilian Personnel Policy and EEO

Irvine H. Dearnley
Vice-President, Citibank, North America, Member, President's Private Sector Survey on Cost Control

Donald J. Devine
Director, Office of Personnel Management

Thomas DeYulia
Majority Staff Director, House Committee on Post Office and Civil Service

Tom Diaz
Columnist, Washington Times

Joseph Dolan
Program Officer, The J. M. Foundation

Martin L. Duggan
Chairman, Advisory Committee on Federal Pay

Herbert E. Ellingwood
Chairman, Merit Systems Protection Board

Andrew A. Feinstein
Staff Director and Chief Counsel, House Subcommittee on Civil Service

A. Lee Fritschler
Director, Center for Public Policy Education, The Brookings Institution

Edward C. Gallas
Vice-President, Organization Resources Counsellors, Inc.

Nesta M. Gallas
Professor of Public Administration, City University of New York

Donald E. Gillis
Chairman of the Board, Professional Managers Association

John M. Golden
Director of Personnel, Office of Personnel and Civil Rights, U.S. Department of Commerce

Edie N. Goldenberg
Associate Professor of Political Science and Public Policy, University of Michigan

Charles T. Goodsell
Center for Public Policy and Administration, Virginia Polytechnic Institute and State University

John D. Harris
Assistant to the National President, American Federation of Government Employees

Robert M. Huberty
Director, Resource Bank, The Heritage Foundation

Dwight A. Ink
Consultant

Peter Katsirubas
Public Service Research Council

Rosslyn S. Kleeman
Associate Director, U.S. General Accounting Office

Jerry D. Klepner
Staff Director, House Subcommittee on Compensation and Employee Benefits

Patrick S. Korten
Executive Assistant Director, Policy and Communications, U.S. Office of Personnel Management

H. James Lawler
Former Director, Corporate Plans, Monsanto Company

Charles H. Levine
Senior Specialist in American National Government and Public Administration, Congressional Research Service

Wesley R. Liebtag
Director, Personnel Programs, IBM

Dennis L. Little
Director, Office of Merit Systems Review and Studies, U.S. Merit Systems Protection Board

Malcolm R. Lovell, Jr.
Guest Scholar, The Brookings Institution

Eugene B. McGregor, Jr.
Professor of Public and Environmental Affairs, Indiana University

Howard M. Messner
Assistant Administrator for Administration, Environmental Protection Agency

James M. Mitchell
Consultant, Center for Public Policy Education, The Brookings Institution

Ronald C. Moe
Specialist in Government Organization and Administration, Congressional Research Service

James W. Morrison, Jr.
Associate Director for Compensation, U.S. Office of Personnel Management

Thomas P. Murphy
Deputy Assistant Secretary for Personnel, U.S. Department of Health and Human Services

Bradley H. Patterson
President, The American Society for Public Administration

B. Guy Peters
Maurice Falk Professor of American Government, University of Pittsburgh

Paul E. Peterson
Director, Governmental Studies Program, The Brookings Institution

John Post
Resident Consultant, The Brookings Institution

Bernard Rosen
Distinguished Adjunct Professor in Residence, The American University

Lois Schutte
Director of Personnel, U.S. Government Printing Office

Barbara L. Schwemle
Analyst in American National Government, Congressional Research Service

Roger B. Semerad
Executive Vice-President, The Brookings Institution

G. Jerry Shaw
Chairman, Public Employees Roundtable; General Counsel, Senior Executives Association

Bruce L. R. Smith
Senior Staff Member, Center for Public Policy Education, The Brookings Institution

Angela M. Specht
Conference Assistant, Center for Public Policy Education, The Brookings Institution

O. Glenn Stahl
Personnel Management Specialist

David T. Stanley
Consultant

Judith L. Tardy
Assistant Secretary for Administration, U.S. Department of Housing and Urban Development